UNDERSTANDING PUBLI

A Contemporary Intro

Edited by
E.K. Sarter and Elizabeth Cookingham Bailey

P

First published in Great Britain in 2023 by

Policy Press, an imprint of
Bristol University Press
University of Bristol
1–9 Old Park Hill
Bristol
BS2 8BB
UK
t: +44 (0)117 374 6645
e: bup-info@bristol.ac.uk

Details of international sales and distribution partners are available at
policy.bristoluniversitypress.co.uk

British Library Cataloguing in Publication Data
A catalogue record for this book is available from the British Library

ISBN 978-1-4473-6399-6 hardcover
ISBN 978-1-4473-6400-9 paperback
ISBN 978-1-4473-6402-3 ePdf
ISBN 978-1-4473-6401-6 ePub

Cover design: Lyn Davies Design
Image credit: Alamy/Mopic
Bristol University Press and Policy Press use environmentally responsible
print partners.
Printed and bound in Great Britain by CPI Group (UK) Ltd, Croydon, CR0 4YY

FSC
www.fsc.org
MIX
Paper | Supporting
responsible forestry
FSC® C013604

To our students past and present

Contents

Contents

List of figures, tables and boxes

Notes on contributors

Wendy Booth is Lecturer in Public Service Management at the University of South Wales, where she has been based for over a decade. She has conducted extensive research into community cohesion and tolerance, and has a keen interest in structural inequalities and their impact on life chances and accessing services.

Elizabeth Cookingham Bailey is Lecturer in Public Policy and Management at the University of York. Her main research interests include the role of voluntary sector organisations in the creation and delivery of social policy, privatisation of education and the development of education policy, and the history of social policy.

Vida Greaux is Lecturer in Social Policy and Public Services at the University of South Wales. Her main interests are in the field of equality and diversity, where she has gained extensive practical and academic experience. She is presently working on the Advance HE Race Equality Charter project on behalf of the University of South Wales.

Stuart Jones is Senior Lecturer in Social Policy and Public Services at the University of South Wales. His research and teaching interests lie in the fields of social policy and public services, community development, sustainability, and the environment.

Jennifer Law is Principal Lecturer in Public Management at the University of South Wales. Her research interests include accountability of public organisations, performance measurement and evaluation, strategy in the public sector, improving public services, and the Well-being of Future Generations Act.

David Phillips is Lecturer in Public Services at the University of South Wales. He has extensive experience working in the third sector and leading small charities. He is particularly interested in the relationship between management and collective leadership within organisations and between them, as well as between service providers and service users (co-production).

Filippos Proedrou is Senior Lecturer in Global Political Economy and Course Leader of the MBA (Master of Business Administration) Global at the University of South Wales, Business School. His research focuses on energy and climate policy, decarbonisation, European Union (EU) studies, EU–Russia relations, and Black Sea and Eastern Mediterranean geopolitics.

Simon Read is Senior Lecturer in Leading Digital Transformation at the University of South Wales. He has vast experience in working in different public services, including the Royal Navy and the Fire Service. His research and teaching interests include project management, law, and emergency and disasters management and response.

E.K. Sarter is Research Fellow/Assistant Professor at the Institute for Employment Research, University of Warwick, with research interests in public and social policies, regulation, multilevel governance and comparative research. Particular areas of interest include employment and the regulation of labour, governance of public services, sustainability, and public procurement as a regulatory tool.

Introduction: Defining and understanding public services

Elizabeth Cookingham Bailey and E.K. Sarter

Be it in France, Greece, Canada, Germany or the UK, emergency ambulances ensure that treatment is quickly available in case of medical emergencies. Publicly provided institutions offer education and the opportunity to learn to everybody. Firefighters respond to crises. Refuse is collected. Youth workers support young people. Public transport opens opportunities to get from one place to another. While these services and their activities and functions differ strongly, all these services can be considered public services.

All of these services fulfil essential tasks in all these – and many other – countries and are in one way or another associated with the state. Consequently, the scope of what constitutes public services is quite broad and will likely differ between countries and over time. Much of the social policy literature focuses on welfare services, or services that deliver **human welfare provision** (Dean, 2012). These tend to be the public services concerned with the delivery of health and social care, education and leisure, social security, and housing. They are complemented with services like fire and rescue, police, and ambulance services, which focus on emergency response as well as providing key preventive programmes. Both welfare and emergency response services are then supported by key regulatory and governance entities, like local authorities, professional bodies and inspectorates. In addition to **soft** (person-centred) services there are **hard services**, such as transportation, waste collection and utilities, which also ensure the needs of the public are met and their rights are maintained. Finally, at the international level, diplomatic and armed forces are public services that protect the rights and interests of individual nation states. However, the wide scope of services covered by the term 'public services' is not the only source of diversity.

While the existence of similar services fulfilling seemingly the same activities and following the same aims in different countries may lead to the assumption that these services are also similar in the ways they are organised and operate, in reality, specific services can differ strongly between countries. They are bound by different legal frameworks and shaped by different sociocultural and political contexts, which influence their goals, their principles of working and their organisational structure. Further, they are organised in very different ways. Take the example of emergency ambulance services, which are an essential service supporting survival in medical emergencies. While emergency medical services exist in all Western countries, their organisation differs vastly. In some countries, they are provided by public bodies themselves. This is, for instance, the case in France, where emergency medical (ambulance) services are provided by the Services d'Aide Médicale Urgente, which forms part of the public system of hospitals. In other countries, the same service may be provided by companies from the private sector or by voluntary (or third) sector organisations. In Denmark, for example, emergency medical services provided by ambulances are either operated by the regions or bought from mainly private providers. Also in Germany, emergency medical services are in some regions provided by non-state actors. However, in contrast to Denmark, in Germany emergency medical services are mostly contracted from voluntary sector organisations, with the Red Cross as the main provider. Thereby, the current provision is bound by earlier organisational choices, which can be characterised by the notion of **path dependence**. This is where previous decisions shape subsequent decisions, making drastic changes rather unlikely. Welfare state institutions and public service organisations become *locked* into ways of operating owing to organisational culture and structure (Pierson, 2000). This *institutional stickiness* can mainly only be broken out of at *critical junctures* (Boettke et al, 2010).

No common terminology exists to refer to these services in cross-country comparison; in different countries and contexts, different terms are used to describe them. While **public services**, the term used in this book (or its literal equivalents such as *services publics*, or *servicios públicos*), is a term used in a range of countries, such as the UK, it is at the same time far from universal. In other settings, these same services come under a range of different labels, such as *services of general interest*. In Germany, where the term public services is uncommon in political, public and academic discourse, the same services are generally referred to as part of *Daseinsvorsorge*.

In brief, these *public services*, *services of general interest*, which form part of *Daseinsvorsorge*, span a broad range of services, are provided in a range of different ways and feature under a variety of names. In the light of this variety and these divergences, the question arises as to what distinguishes these public services, which is the term used in this book, from other services. In other words, the very starting point for any exploration of public services is understanding the meaning of the term itself and identifying those distinctive features that characterise a public service.

Defining public services

Carrying on from the example of emergency medical services, which are provided by different organisations in different countries, public services are not necessarily provided by the state and its agencies themselves. They can be provided by public, private or voluntary sector organisations. Public sector organisations are those that are both operated and funded by governments. Private sector organisations are generally companies with a profit motive. Voluntary sector organisations are neither part of nor operated by the state nor are they operating based on a profit motive; they tend to be organisations operating to foster certain social, environmental or cultural goals, such as charities or community initiatives. When providing public services, private and voluntary sector organisations may have access to government funding, for example, based on contracts for the delivery of specific services. (Traditionally many welfare services are also provided informally through local networks or families; however, this book, like the term public services itself, refers to the formal delivery of public services.) When these services are not provided directly by the state and its agencies, then their delivery has been delegated to organisations from the private or voluntary sector, who are in turn receiving public funding to deliver them. Regardless of whether these essential services are provided by a public, a voluntary or a private organisation, public services are provided *by or on behalf of the government and the public sector*.

Public service functions

While some services are completely left to the market and neither provided nor funded by the government, others are provided on behalf of the government; this is because they are considered to *fulfil essential functions*, which are vital for society and the state. These essential functions can broadly be classed in two categories: meeting essential needs and ensuring that rights are met. As Titmuss noted, public services (or specifically social services) 'are concerned with delivering and providing services to meet publicly acknowledged needs which markets or the family cannot, or should not, or will not, meet' (Titmuss, 1974: 52). The following will explore what **needs** are and examine the different *definitions of need* which can determine the aims of public services.

A **basic need** is something that must be met for people to survive, like food or shelter. Pointing beyond the idea of basic needs is the question asked by Dean (2010) of what an **absolute need** is – something that is understood as basic to all human survival regardless of context. While food and shelter might then be both absolute and basic needs, there are other needs which might be considered basic depending on the context; these are **relative needs** (Bradshaw, 1972; Dean, 2010). This then also leads to the crucial differentiation between **individual needs**, such as what each individual person may need for their specific life, and those **social needs** that are relevant for society as a whole (Bradshaw, 1972). Public services fulfil social needs. One core debate in social policy is how to measure the *extent of need*. Bradshaw (1972) provides a framework for understanding the range of different ways in which one could understand social needs: *felt needs* are those needs of which individuals are aware. *Normative needs* are those which are defined by those in positions of authority. *Expressed needs* are those that are articulated by the individuals themselves, for example to public services. Finally, *comparative needs* are those that one feels in relation to other groups, normally resulting from a lack of something compared to another. If needs are so hard to define, this raises the question of which needs are most basic or absolute and are understood inherently by people, and how can those be satisfied (Doyal and Gough, 1991; Dean, 2010).

Do public services only address these basic needs? What about those needs which are only identified because of external influences, comparative or relative needs? It is quite hard to determine the theoretical or moral limits of public service delivery in relation to meeting needs. In practice, public services are limited by the resources they have available to address needs; the way those resources are determined depends on culture, history and ideology. This also means that the extent to which needs are met by or on behalf of the state (as opposed to the market) is largely determined by the cultural and ideological perspective of a country and the welfare state structure.

Dean (2010; 2012) provides a useful framework that situates different approaches to meeting needs by governments on a spectrum of (more) individualistic or solidaristic ideologies. He also locates ideologies between those that are more inclined to maintain the status quo (*conservative*) and those that seek to address inequalities (*egalitarian*) (Dean, 2010; 2012). The positioning on these two spectra shapes how different welfare states approach needs and the extent to which they are met. More socially progressive states might take quite a broad idea of the interventions that the state undertakes to meet citizen needs. In contrast, more conservative welfare states may wish to take a more *paternalistic* approach to meeting the needs that ensure continuous participation in the social order (Dean, 2010; 2012).

Based on the way that welfare states, economies and labour markets were set up and which actors were relevant forces for shaping welfare states, Esping-Andersen (1990) created a typology of Western welfare regimes. Despite discussions on whether the original three regimes capture the breadth of reality or should be enhanced by further regimes to account for the specificities of, for example, Mediterranean or Eastern European states, this typology is also helpful for understanding how welfare states meet needs. *Liberal welfare states* rely on a strong role for the market and have relatively basic welfare provision, which often is means-tested. Based on a historical corporatist and statist tradition, *Conservative welfare states* focus on upholding differentiated status. *Social-democratic welfare states* have a rather egalitarian approach: they deliver welfare that is relatively universal in coverage and less linked to employment. These different approaches to constructing welfare states show that there are a range of ways of meeting needs which public services adhere to.

Closely linked to how needs are defined and consequently how they are met by public services, is the consideration of citizens' or residents' rights within a country, which shape how they access public services to meet those needs. Marshall (1992) provides one of the key frameworks for understanding social rights, but again draws on a Western historical account of the evolution of citizenship rights and freedoms. This has led to an understanding of citizenship and rights in three parts: first, *civil rights and citizenship*, which includes personal freedoms and legal rights; second, *political rights and citizenship*, which include democratic freedoms and electoral rights; and third, *social rights and citizenship*, which include freedom from necessity and the extension of welfare rights. Public services tend to focus primarily on ensuring social rights; yet they also relate to issues of civil rights. The degree to which individual responsibilities are attached to citizens exercising those rights is also a consideration of social policy. Citizens, and to a certain extent residents, have the right to access certain services (to meet their needs) but owing to ideological influences on the welfare state, or resource constraints within states, they must also fulfil certain obligations to obtain those services. The moral and logistical issues of both ensuring rights are upheld and enforcing associated responsibilities are frequently issues for public services.

Public service functions and the policy process

As noted earlier, different ideological approaches are crucial for shaping an individual state's actions. This is important because not all needs which can be identified are addressed by public services. Rather, some needs are addressed by the state while others are delegated to the market or are not addressed at all by formal services. Consequently, the decision of whether a specific need is to be addressed by public action, or a right upheld, is a fundamentally political question. The selection of the needs that are met by services provided by or on behalf of the state, as well as the guidelines for how to meet them, is best understood through a policy lens. The formulation of policies involves the selection of ideas, setting of agendas and decision making. Kingdon (2003) describes the creation of policies as picking between a range of problems to address and between possible solutions. This also means that in the process of policymaking, different needs and problems may be considered. The possible needs that exist in a society and the possible ways of ensuring rights are met can be described as different **policy ideas**. Hall (1993) describes these as the problems or goals that policies try to address and different tools that might be used to do so. The way in which certain ideas are selected for public attention (for example by publicly delivering services in relation to them) is largely determined by the influence of different actors. Actors constitute the people and groups that influence the acceptance of ideas. These groups can be professional bodies associated with specific public services, interest groups promoting a particular need or right, or experts with core knowledge. They are sources of expertise and key to generating new ideas. Groups or individuals who promote policies constitute **policy entrepreneurs** (Goldstein and Keohane, 1993; Béland, 2005).

Individuals and groups might be integrated in informal or formal ways into decision making regarding public policies. They may be involved through consultations, which is a more open process by which governments ask for a variety of groups to provide ideas. They may be involved through more closed processes, like debates or hearings, where specific experts are asked to comment on issues. Interest groups can also be more proactive rather than reactive by lobbying for specific rights or drafting publications which highlight needs. These different ways of integrating interests into the selection of ideas depend on the decision-making models used. The more **rational model** might take a very open consultation approach to consider all possible problems and solutions (Simon, 1947). In contrast, the more **incremental model** might rely on specific hearings and debates to cope with issues as they emerge (Lindblom, 1959; 1979). In short, this all means that public services are fundamentally grounded in public policy and political desire to promote certain social policy goals, which are negotiated by different actors.

Bringing all these aspects together, a definition of public services emerges: public services are services provided by or on behalf of the state to individuals, families and communities to meet or satisfy needs, which based on political decisions are deemed to warrant public action.

Public services and social policy

Public services are intrinsically linked to and embedded in social policy. Social policy encompasses all the social structures which shape individual and societal wellbeing. Public services are but one, yet important, aspect within the broader net of social policy. They are an essential part of the delivery of social policy; the mechanism by which larger social policy ideas are achieved.

At the same time as being interrelated with but distinct from social policy, public services are related to but at the same time different from the public sector. In a UK context, the term **public sector** captures 'those parts of the economy that are either in state ownership or under contract to the state, plus those parts that are regulated and/or subsidized in the public interest' (Flynn, 2007: 2). In contrast, the term **public services** means those services which are provided to the public by or on behalf of the state, whether they are provided by or funded and regulated by the state and its agencies. Public services are also not solely concerned with public administration. Public administration in many countries focuses on the role of the civil service in the delivery of social policy. Therefore, public administration largely sits within public services, while the latter contains the wider range of frontline service work that ensures human wellbeing.

Overview of book

Having defined public services as services, which based on political decisions are provided by or on behalf of the state to individuals, families and communities to meet or satisfy needs, this book will explore the context, structure and management of these services, as well as key issues and challenges.

Taking the notion that public services do not exist in a vacuum but are embedded in the broader context of the (welfare) state and shaped by a multitude of external factors, Part I, 'Public services and the welfare state', explores ways of understanding the larger political and legal frameworks in which public services operate. Chapter 1 ('Public services and public policies') explores public policies and their relationship to public services. It shows that public services are not only grounded in political decisions but also shaped by public and social policies, which are important forces impacting public service goals, delivery and impact. Starting by exploring policies as one aspect of the political, this chapter examines the policy process and showcases the crucial importance of actors and ideas in making and implementing policies. As this chapter shows, the relationship between public policies and public services is not limited to the impact that public policies have on public services. Once a public policy or a political decision that concerns public services has been made, it must be implemented to have an effect in reality. Policies provide a framework that conveys a certain discretion to those engaged in their implementation, who interpret policy goals and principles and choose specific ways to implement a policy into action. Public services are essential actors in the implementation of many public policies. Individual actors, in this case public service professionals and street-level bureaucrats, are of crucial importance, especially in person-centred services. The choices made in the implementation have crucial impacts on the policy outcomes achieved. Consequently, as key actors in the implementation, public services are also crucial agents in shaping public policies and their impact. This chapter furthermore shows that the implementation of policies by public services is far from a uniform process. Several factors may influence the effectiveness of the implementation, including the complexity of the issue, the scale and scope of the change, and the resource requirements.

Having explored the policy process and the relationship between public policies and public services, Chapter 2 ('Mixed economy') turns to examine the variety of sectors that provide public services and implement those policies. Each sector has a distinctive culture and motivation which also determines how public services in each sector approach the implementation of policies. This chapter seeks to showcase the benefits of the mixed provision of welfare over time, particularly in welfare services, and the long history of voluntary action in the emergency services, such as community policing and volunteer firefighters in rural communities. The chapter also shows that to deal with new risks and changing political agendas, a more collaborative approach that draws on the skills of different sectors is essential to deliver effective public services. This also requires clear regulation and legal contracts to ensure the effective management of these relationships. As Chapter 3 ('Public services and the law') outlines, the legal framework that governs public services is complex and is built from a mix of supranational, national, regional and local law. This chapter focuses on the connections between different legal documents, such as treaties, resolutions, statutes, common law and byelaws, and examines their impacts on public services. This chapter shows the importance of international organisations, such as the United Nations, the European Union and the World Trade Organization, in setting the public service legal framework. It also examines the important role of legal entities, like the International Criminal Court and the International Court of Justice, in shaping public service law. Alongside the importance of international entities in shaping the legal framework that surrounds public services, this chapter looks at the specific role of national and regional governments in law-making, using the UK and its devolved nations as examples.

Based on an understanding of these larger contextual factors, Part II, 'The internal dynamics of public services', turns to how those managing and leading public services translate these external factors into how services operate. Chapter 4 ('Organisations and institutions') explores how external political, economic and social influences shape organisations. It draws on principles of institutional analysis and the importance of historical legacies to explain how and why public service organisations change. The competing external forces that drive that change (political, economic and social) are outlined before turning to how managers and leaders seek to manage that change internally. Hereby, this chapter considers the internal dynamics of organisations and the importance of actors in shaping the implementation of these external policies and setting the internal direction of organisations.

Bringing about change requires strategic thinking and management and leadership which incorporates both short- and long-term planning. Chapter 5 ('Strategy and strategic management') explores the various concepts of strategy and the role of strategy in making successful organisations, including understanding how decision makers anticipate the future, engage stakeholders, and look for creative and innovative solutions. The chapter explores the importance of the environment, the strategic choices that organisations can make, and the different types of processes (rational and emergent) that they use. Then, Chapter 6 ('Leadership and management') covers the development of modern management and leadership styles from their classical origins. It contrasts different views of the relationship between public sector managers and leaders and the people they work with. It looks at the distinction between management, with an emphasis on procedure and structure, and leadership, with an emphasis on motivation and the alignment of organisational and personal values. The chapter concludes with a look at future trends and argues that management and leadership are different, but equally important, skill sets.

Based on the examination of the broader environment and internal dynamics, Part III, 'Achieving social and environmental impact', focuses on current and emerging topics, which deeply impact the way public services operate and are provided. Sustainability is an increasingly important concern. Chapter 7 ('Public services and the challenge of sustainability') shows that, while initially focused on agriculture, sustainability has increasingly broadened its scope and is today commonly understood as a multidimensional concept comprising economic, environmental and social aspects. This chapter examines the drive towards sustainability and outlines key challenges. With recourse to an important activity relating to public services, public procurement, this chapter exemplifies the tension between financial and environmental and social aspects.

Chapter 8 ('Public services and equality') explores one aspect of the social dimension of sustainability. It examines key ideas about equality and diversity, as deployed in contemporary policy, theory and discourse, and examines why and how these ideas matter for public services. The starting point is the idea that inequality exists, and that public services are concerned with inequality for a variety of reasons, from normative reasons and legal obligations to concerns about their ability to meet their goals. This chapter shows that by virtue of the way they are distributed, the way they treat people and the outcomes they help produce, public services have a material impact on equality.

Chapter 9 ('Public services and the environmental crisis') explores the environmental dimension of sustainability as an emerging challenge. This chapter outlines the environmental crisis from the perspective of a social problem, which is a problem that is both caused by human societies and presents fundamental challenges for future patterns of life. The chapter begins with a brief consideration of the nature of the environmental crisis before briefly mapping its key social dimensions and dynamics. It then turns its attention to some of the implications for public services. In doing so it argues that the environmental crisis not only requires public services to adapt but also requires a fundamental rethink of how public services are organised and delivered. It furthermore showcases that public services can contribute to the systemic changes required in the quest for a sustainable future.

Finally, Chapter 10 ('Adapting organisations: public services, climate change and the energy transition') brings many of the ideas discussed in the first nine chapters, particularly those in Parts I and II, together to focus on how public services can innovate and adapt to address contemporary and future challenges. This chapter focuses on how public services adapt in the era of the unprecedented challenge of climate change. More specifically, it examines energy-related functions of public services actors and outlines how these can contribute to facilitating an energy transition as part of a response to climate change. These functions include, among others, planning competences, setting of standards, and regulatory functions, as well as entrepreneurial-like activities such as energy generation, co-production and trade. This chapter raises questions regarding the ways and the extent to which public services adapt their functions and strategies in a climate burdened world and to the appropriate balance between marketisation and public provision of public services. Finally, it assesses the degree to which public services provision adjusts to climate change concerns. This chapter in particular highlights the challenges that public services are facing across several areas, but it also provides some potential solutions.

The conclusion brings together key aspects, trends and developments from all chapters and explores their implications for public services in the future. It thereby focuses particularly on how public services, and public servants, will need to adapt for the 21st century.

Language use

Language is more than a mere means of conveying information; words are important, they can carry pejorative and harmful connotations. Over the past years and decades, many countries have seen debates about terms and terminologies, one example of which is presented in Box 8.1 in Chapter 8. Throughout this book, the language used is intended to avoid pejorative terminology and reflect to the best of our knowledge preferred self-identification of the organisations or individuals discussed. Yet, terms for self-identification differ between countries and may diverge between individuals. Guided by recent debates in the UK, this book uses **Black** to refer to individuals whose lived experiences are shaped by experiences of structural disadvantages and discrimination based on their skin colour. **Ethnic minorities** refers to people who are part of a cultural minority group. **Deaf** (with a capital D) is used to refer to people who have a hearing impairment and identify as Deaf and with the Deaf community. Additionally, where appropriate, the terminology for a public service or a specific institution may also be expressed in the native language accompanied by an English translation.

Pedagogical features

Each chapter contains elements to aid the use of this textbook for both teaching and learning. The key content chapters (Chapters 1 to 10) each begin with a textbox ('chapter objectives'), which outlines key elements discussed in the chapter, and end with a list of key points that stress the most important learning points from the chapter. Throughout the chapters, when important general concepts are first introduced, they are highlighted in bold. Additionally, key concepts of a particular author are highlighted in italics. To enable testing understanding of the content of the chapter and aid classroom discussions, a list of questions are included at the end, which explore ideas introduced in the chapter. A list of further readings are outlined at the end of each chapter, which point to additional sources that allow greater exploration of specific areas.

References

Béland, D. (2005) 'Ideas and social policy: An institutionalist perspective', *Social Policy and Administration*, 39(1): 1–18.

Boettke, P.J., Coyne, C.J. and Leeson, P.T. (2010) 'Institutional stickiness and the new development economics', *American Journal of Economics and Sociology*, 67(2): 331–358.

Bradshaw, J.R. (1972) 'The taxonomy of social need', in McLachlan, G. (ed.), *Problems and progress in medical care*, Oxford: Oxford University Press, pp 71–82.

Dean, H. (2010) *Understanding human need: Social issues, policy and practice*, Bristol: Policy Press.

Dean, H. (2012) *Social policy* (2nd edn), Cambridge: Polity Press.

Doyal, L. and Gough, L. (1991) *A theory of human need*, Basingstoke: Macmillan.

Esping-Andersen, G. (1990) *The three worlds of welfare capitalism*, Cambridge: Polity Press.

Flynn, N. (2007) *Public sector management*, London: SAGE.

Goldstein, J. and Keohane, R.O. (eds) (1993) *Ideas and foreign policy: Beliefs, institutions, and political change*, Ithaca: Cornell University Press.

Hall, P.A. (1993) 'Policy paradigms, social learning, and the state: The case of economic policymaking in Britain', *Comparative Politics*, 25(3): 275–296.

Kingdon, J.W. (2003) *Agendas, alternatives, and public policies*, New York: Longman.

Lindblom, C.E. (1959) 'The science of "muddling through"', *Public Administration Review*, 19(2): 79–88.

Lindblom, C.E. (1979) 'Still muddling, not yet through', *Public Administration Review*, 39(6): 517–526.

Marshall, T.H. (1992) *Citizenship and social class*, London: Pluto Press.

Pierson, P. (2000) 'Increasing returns, path dependence, and the study of politics', *The American Political Science Review*, 94(2): 251–267.

Simon, H.A. (1947) *Administrative behavior: A study of decision-making processes in administrative organization* (1st edn), New York: The Macmillan Company.

Titmuss, R.M. (1974) *Social policy: An introduction*, London: George Allen & Unwin.

PART I

Public services and the welfare state

1

Public services and public policies

E.K. Sarter

Chapter objectives

Policies are targeted plans or courses of action which are devised, installed and carried out to resolve a specific issue. Public policies are those policies devised and adopted by public actors. This chapter explores the policy process with a particular focus on policy implementation. It shows that public policies shape public services, their goals, delivery and organisation. This chapter furthermore shows how public services shape policy outcomes. Public services, and those working within them, are essential agents for the implementation of policies. By virtue of their involvement in the implementation of policies, public services are crucial for shaping policy outcomes.

Introduction

From emergency services such as the police and ambulance services to welfare services, public services provide essential services, without which we cannot imagine modern welfare states. Thereby, public services do not exist in a vacuum. They are embedded in the broader political and economic context, a legal framework, and a specific cultural and social environment.

Public policies in particular are crucial for shaping public services because they define the aims and goals public services seek to achieve, influence their ways of working and structure their interaction with members of the public. Policies are one part of the political; the realm of the political is composed of three core parts, polity, politics and policies, which – while interrelated – take a specific focus in distinct aspects of the political. **Polity** refers to the institutional structures that taken together form the political system. **Politics** relates to procedural aspects, or processes. **Policy**, in contrast, denotes the content-related aspect of the political. To understand the distinction, take the example of the environment. Environmental policy relates to the content, ideas, goals and rules, as they relate to the environment, while politics refers to the processes that enable these contents to emerge and form a part of reality. Polity in turn refers to the structures in and through which these policies see the light of day.

A variety of definitions exists for policies, the focus of this chapter. These share a set of core features, namely the idea that policies are a targeted plan or course of action which is devised, installed and carried out to resolve a specific issue. These issues can be existing problems or concerns about anticipated or identified trends or developments. Policies then can be understood as a plan or course of action devised in response to an existing or anticipated issue, concern or problem, set out and followed by an actor or a range of actors. Public policies are those policies devised by public actors and government bodies most importantly. They can focus on regulation (regulatory policies), on the distribution or redistribution of resources (distributive or redistributive policies respectively), or aim to create or change state institutions (constituent policies).

Public policies shape the goals of public services and their ways of working; they commit public services to specific goals and lay down principles to which public services must adhere. Policies mould the organisational structure of public services and shape their inner workings. While public policies are a crucial force shaping public services, the relationship between public policies and public services is not one-sided. As shown in this chapter, public services are key actors that put policies into practice. Particularly **street–level bureaucrats** (Lipsky, 1980), those working in public service roles where they have direct interaction with members of the public and hold discretion, are of key importance. By virtue of being essential agents in the implementation, public services (and street–level bureaucrats in particular) shape policy outcomes, for instance by deciding on specific ways to implement a policy and to operationalise broader policy goals.

Before exploring the importance of public services for putting policies into practice in more detail, it is essential to first explore the **policy process**; that is, the process through which policies are made, implemented and assessed. Based on the exploration of public policies, this chapter turns its attention to public services and their interaction with public policies more specifically. Following a brief outline of the importance that public policies have for public services, this chapter explores the role of public services in the implementation of public policies and examines their impact for shaping policy outcomes. To conclude, trends and developments are outlined.

The policy process

Usually, the origins of current thinking about the policy process are traced back to Lasswell (1956), who proposed a seven-stage model of the policy process, comprising: intelligence, promotion, prescription, invocation, application, termination and appraisal. While the specific model of the policy process has been contested, the model became the starting point for a broader discussion and the creation of a variety of typologies of the policy process. Today, different conceptualisations of the policy process exist, which can be grouped into linear models on the one hand and a cyclical understanding of the policy process (the so-called policy cycle) on the other. These have both commonalities and differences. Both **linear models** and the **policy cycle** share the idea that the policy process encompasses a set of distinct steps. They differ in how they envision the relationship between these stages. Linear models do not account for the possibility of feedback loops or a development other than a linear progression. While linear models tend to see the policymaking process as a linear way to transform inputs (for instance in the form of public demand) into policy outputs, the policy cycle envisions policymaking as a continuous process. Since the 1970s, the accuracy of the rational-technical model of policymaking, which understands policymaking using a straightforward model, where inputs are transformed into outputs, was increasingly questioned and cyclical models of the policy process gained importance. Today, there is not one single model but a range of conceptualisations, which feature some common stages that are outlined in the following (see Figure 1.1). When considering the policy cycle, it is crucial to acknowledge that conceptualisations of the policy process are heuristic models, which aim at providing generalised insights. It is vital to highlight that as such they do not necessarily always present a straightforward reflection of reality. In practice, different steps may not be clearly delineated, or steps may be missing.

Taking the definition of a policy as a plan or course of action devised in response to an existing or anticipated issue, concern or problem, which is set out and followed by an actor or a range of actors, as a starting point, it is obvious that any policy is a response to an issue deemed to require attention.

Figure 1.1: The policy cycle

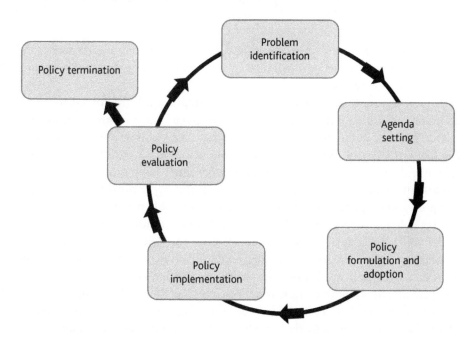

Consequently, the very first stage in the life of any policy is the identification of an existing or anticipated issue, concern or problem, which needs to be addressed (**problem recognition**). Problem recognition entails two essential components. The first is the identification of a specific phenomenon, trend or development. This depends on the identification of evidence, (empirical) data or projections. Yet the identification of an issue, trend or development is not on its own sufficient for the identification of a *problem*. The identification of a problem requires not only the recognition of a fact but also the identification of this fact or phenomenon as a problem. This means that problem recognition relies on the identification of a phenomenon *and* the (individual and/or collective) assessment and appraisal of this fact as an occurrence which is less than desirable (a problem) and which warrants action to rectify or improve it. In particular, the identification of a phenomenon as a problem and the assessment that this problem merits attention depends on (individual and/or collective) judgement, which in turn is based on values, beliefs and priorities that actors hold. Spector and Kitsuse argue that it is through the process of claiming a problem that an issue comes to be (perceived as) a problem:

> [T]he evidence that there is, for example, a crime problem is not that there is a high rate of crime or that the rate is higher than it used to be. Rather the evidence is that there are many individuals and groups complaining about various aspects of crime – violence in the streets, burglaries in the suburbs, corruption in the police force, etc. – and the activities of the myriad agencies that are mandated to do something about those complaints. (Spector and Kitsuse, 1973: 158)

Taken in this sense, problem recognition is a deeply social act of recognising and assessing reality, comparing it to a desired state, and assessing whether it requires attention by policymakers.

While identifying a problem is an essential step towards the formulation and adoption of a policy, it is not sufficient. At any given time, various actors identify a wide range of different problems, which they assess as warranting attention in the form of a policy (Kingdon, 1984). With a multitude of different problems (combined with a range of different and oftentimes contrasting or conflicting assessments of the issues in question), not everything identified by actors results in a policy. For a policy to be made, the identified problem needs to find its place on the political agenda (**agenda setting**). Agenda setting is the essential stage in the policy cycle during which those problems that will proceed to give life to a policy are separated from those that remain unaddressed. It can be visualised as an arena where a vast number of problems (and actors advocating for them) compete for attention; only those issues that are successful in this competition will proceed to give rise to a policy. The success in this competition for a place on the political agenda is shaped by the availability of one or more possible solutions and the political climate at the specific time (Kingdon, 1984: 93). The influence and strategies of policy actors within the given political system are core to whether a problem is placed on the agenda.

Once a problem has been identified and successfully placed on the agenda, a specific policy to address it is formulated (**policy formulation**) and adopted (**policy adoption**). Here, the focus turns from the question of *which* issue needs to be addressed to *how* it should be addressed. Like problem identification, the formulation of a policy is shaped by the influence of actors and their beliefs, values and priorities. Different actors perceive different outcomes as sensible, desirable and preferable, which results in different ideas about the specific goals of a policy and, consequently, different ideas for policies (Hall, 1993; Campbell, 2002; Béland, 2005). In the policy formulation stage, different alternatives for routes of action are considered and weighed up, for instance in public consultations (see Introduction). This leads to the decision for, and subsequently the adoption of, one of these alternative routes of action. Like in the previous step, agenda setting, the definition of the aim and the decision for a specific approach is shaped by the influence of actors, who, based on similar understandings of reality, values and beliefs, can come together to form coalitions to strengthen their standing.

Once a specific policy is decided and adopted, it must be put into practice – it must be implemented (**policy implementation**). Policy implementation is the bridge between the policy and its effects on the ground; it is an essential stage in the policy process that brings a policy to life and a crucial step for achieving and shaping policy outcomes. Public policies provide a framework that leaves scope for interpretation and clarification of the specific goals they set out, and ways to achieve them. These are defined in the implementation (Sabatier and Mazmanian, 1980). The implementation stage is a major stage for public services' involvement in a policy's lifecycle, explored in the subsection on public services and the implementation of public policies later in this chapter. Street-level bureaucrats are of particular importance in the implementation of many public policies (Lipsky, 1980).

To know whether a policy has achieved its goals and to assess desired and/or undesired impacts that resulted from its implementation, **policy evaluation** is crucial. It consists of systematically collecting and analysing evidence and data to assess the context, actions and outcomes of the policy and its implementation. Policy evaluation can draw on a range of quantitative and qualitative empirical research methods to understand whether a policy succeeded in supporting the aims it set out to achieve and whether, where and why it may have fallen short of achieving these goals. If the goal of a specific policy is, for instance, to increase recycling in a specific area, the evaluation of the policy will assess whether recycling rates in the area have increased (and to what degree) or not. Further, an evaluation may seek to identify reasons for the success or failure of a policy and potential areas of improvement. Depending on the outcomes of the assessment of the impact of the policy, policy evaluation can lead to sustaining the policy or to **policy termination** (if it was successful), or it can mark the beginning of a new cycle, which seeks to address and alleviate remaining problems.

Actors and ideas

Having explored the policy process, the crucial importance of actors throughout it has become obvious. **Actors** are active subjects that shape the policy process, from the identification of a problem to the implementation of policies. The aim of an actor's involvement in a policy process is to translate ideas and beliefs into policies to help shape reality in accordance with their ideas, beliefs and values. To strengthen their influence, actors form alliances or coalitions with other actors who share similar ideas and aims (Sabatier, 1988). These coalitions can be formal or informal and range from short-term alliances to support very specific ideas and aims on a single occasion to long-term coalitions. The ability of actors and coalitions to transfer their ideas into policies depends on a range of factors, including the position actors hold in the specific political system and the policy field in question, the pressure they can exert, and their strategy and skills in advocating their position. Depending on the specific stage of the policy process, different actors will be involved.

Actors' priorities and actions are shaped by **ideas** and beliefs about how the world should be, what is important, and what should be addressed by policy (and how). Consequently, ideas are crucial for the policy process; they shape what different actors perceive as a problem and what they deem necessary to be tackled and addressed by a policy (Kingdon, 1984). Ideas and beliefs shape the priorities different actors hold; they influence which issues actors advocate to place on the agenda, the goals they advocate for policies, and the ways they advocate for these to be addressed. Values and beliefs are not just individual ideas attached to individual policymakers; they relate back to culture. **Culture** can be defined as transmitted patterns of interpretation (Geertz, 1973). It shapes an individual's understanding and interpretation of the world as well as their values, ideas and beliefs. It thereby also shapes how policymakers interpret the world and which values, ideas and beliefs they hold. Beliefs and values are rather persistent; cultural change, while an important influence, is a rather slow process (Inglehart, 1990). Consequently, when compared cross-nationally, political processes and policies may reflect different cultural influences on interpretations and ideas, which shape actors' ideas, values and paradigms, and thereby policies.

Conflicting goals and wicked issues

While policies are a plan or course of action devised in response to an existing or anticipated issue, set out and followed by actors, their creation and implementation is not always straightforward.

First, no policy stands in isolation; rather, every policy is part of a wider and interconnected web of policies, which address a specific part of a complex web of multifaceted issues. Focusing on different policy fields, policies can lay out different goals. Furthermore, different policy goals can be contained in one policy. Those formulating and implementing policies therefore navigate a complex field of aims, goals, opportunities and constraints, which may be difficult to reconcile (see Chapter 7). As the case of the M4 (see Box 1.1) highlights, when faced with diverse implications of a proposed action, these different aspects need to be weighed against each other to decide whether and how to pursue an action or a project.

Box 1.1: The M4 relief road

The M4 relief road was a proposed construction project in South Wales, which aimed to relieve traffic congestion on the M4. The Welsh Government assessed its impacts against set policy goals including: to promote regional economic development and employment opportunities, protect national heritage, safeguard the environment and conserve wildlife. The economic assessment of this project suggested that the construction of the relief road would reduce travel times and improve access to the area. This in turn would facilitate South Wales' businesses more effectively accessing domestic and international markets, generating a positive impact for the Welsh tourism industry and improving access to employment opportunities. While the projected economic impact was beneficial, concerns were raised over the impact on other policy objectives, most importantly on the historic and ecological environment and biodiversity. Affecting an area of Outstanding Historic Interest and an important and protected site for wildlife (the Gwent Levels), the proposed road would have had adverse environmental impacts and negative implications for biodiversity. Additionally, it would involve the demolition of historic sites with implications for in the UK further archaeological discoveries.

In addition to conflicting goals, public policies face highly complex issues, whose interwoven nature poses serious problems for their resolution. In the 1970s, when the rational-technical model of policy was increasingly questioned, the idea and the concept of so-called **wicked issues** or problems gained increasing attention. In contrast to **tame problems**, which are relatively easy to define and address, wicked issues are highly complex and hard to conceptualise, understand, tackle and solve.

Rittel and Webber (1973) define wicked problems as extraordinarily complex issues. In contrast to tame problems, which can be clearly and exhaustively formulated in a way that contains all the information necessary for their solution, wicked issues cannot be conclusively described. While wicked problems may display similarities to other problems, they may also possess distinguishing features that make them unique. Further, every wicked problem can also be understood as part of another problem. No clear principles or rules exist that can identify its root cause. Take the example of crime: no one clear cause of criminal behaviour exists. Rather crime and crime rates are shaped by a range of interacting features, from unemployment and poverty to alcohol and drug abuse, and housing policy. With a multitude of factors influencing crime and crime rates, no one single root cause can be identified.

In a way, the inability to formulate a wicked issue in a comprehensive manner is part of the problem itself, as problems of understanding a wicked issue translate into the process of solving it. The higher the number of factors that contribute to an issue, the harder it is to identify a way to solve the problem. Closely linked to the underlying problem of defining a wicked problem and identifying a way to address it is the fact that there is no clear rule on how to identify solutions to wicked problems. There is no defined and enumerable set of possible solutions which can be taken as a starting point for defining a plan of action. Several interested parties can evaluate solutions and label them as better or worse according to the parties' specific interests, values or priorities; no clear rule for establishing the correctness of a solution exists and no one party has the authority to set such a rule. Returning to the example of crime, some actors may focus on a tough stance against crime by increasing the number of police officers or introducing tougher punishments. In contrast, other actors may focus on combating poverty, creating more integrative and mixed neighbourhoods, and so on.

In addition, wicked issues and the actions used to tackle them have important real-life impacts and any attempt to tackle a wicked issue by implementing a course of action will change aspects of reality. This will then change the situation, which may subsequently require a different solution. Consequently, (potential) solutions which may be helpful for tackling wicked issues cannot be tested before they are applied. This becomes rather obvious when looking at the example of crime. Any measure that is introduced to fight crime will alter reality, be it actions to combat poverty, tougher laws and so on. Solving a wicked issue is, therefore, a 'one-shot operation' (Rittel and Webber, 1973: 163). Lastly, no stopping rules exist, so it is difficult to identify the point at which an issue has been resolved. In brief, wicked issues, oftentimes encountered by public services, 'defy efforts to delineate their boundaries and to identify their causes, and thus to expose their problematic nature' (Rittel and Webber, 1973: 167).

Taken together, these inherent features of wicked issues create a highly complex situation besieged with uncertainties. Combined with gaps in knowledge, the lack of a clear understanding of the problem leads to uncertainty around the substance of the problem. The fact that many actors are involved, who display different preferences and value sets, who are embedded in a range of networks, organisations and so on, and who often act in unpredictable ways, adds a further layer of complexity. Further, due to the complexity and the instability of wicked issues, as well as the uncertainties regarding their formulation and the ways to tackle it, tackling a wicked issue often generates unpredicted consequences. For instance, in the UK, academies were originally advocated and introduced to improve education in poorer areas. Yet after the introduction of these schools, some selection criteria (normally based on specialist subjects) were introduced and it became harder for the same pupils to gain admission.

Public services and public policies

Public services can be the object of a policy as well as an active subject, an actor, in a policy process. In other words, public services can be shaped by policies and shape public policy outcomes. The following explores how public policies shape public services before turning to how public services, as active agents in the implementation of policies, shape policy outcomes.

As has been outlined in this chapter, public policies set goals, aims, principles and a regulatory framework, all of which have important implications for public services. When defining policy goals and broader principles that touch upon the areas and work of public services, public policies define their goals and aims and commit them to certain principles. By setting out the broader framework within which public services operate, public policies have further implications for the organisational structure, the internal workings and the funding of public services (see Chapters 2, 4 and 5). Take the example of the Well-being of Future Generations (Wales) Act 2015 (see Chapter 7). This act commits public bodies to work towards more sustainable practices. This has important implications for public services, who must assess and evaluate their practices, identify room for improvement, and adjust their practice to better align with the goals set out in this act. At the same time, it commits these public bodies to adopt specific ways of working, which means reassessing the ways in which these organisations work internally (see Chapter 5) and engaging with other actors. Likewise, the Nolan Principles, which commit those working in the public sector in the UK to adhere to specific ethical standards or targets (see Chapter 4), have deep implications for public services and those working within them. In brief, public policies exert an important influence not only on the goals public services set out to achieve but also on how they aim to achieve them.

Public services and the implementation of public policies

Yet the relationship between public policies and public services is not unilateral; not only do public policies exert an important impact on public services, but public services are in turn crucial agents shaping the implementation of public policies and their outcomes. Public services can be involved at various stages of the policy process; they can, for instance, contribute to the identification of a problem by gathering and providing data, providing evidence and drawing attention to problems. Yet their most important and structurally embedded role is in the implementation of public policies, which is at the same time crucial for shaping policy outcomes and the key stage for public services' involvement. In the following, the role and importance of public services in the implementation of policies will be the focus of interest.

While public policies define a framework and goals, neither the framework nor the goals by themselves have a direct impact on reality. To affect and influence reality, policies must be implemented. Public policies provide goals, aims and a set of rules, which form a framework that defines core aspects but leaves some crucial details to be interpreted and important aspects to be worked out in (and for) their implementation (Hill and Hupe, 2002). Public services are important actors in the implementation. They enjoy a certain freedom (or **discretion**) to interpret and specify aspects of a policy, to choose one way of implementing a policy over other available alternatives, a freedom that has important real-life impacts. Through their involvement in the implementation of policies, public services and those working in them exert an important influence on the interpretation of policies and on their outcomes.

At the same time as having the discretion to interpret goals and policies and to devise and carry out a way to implement policies, those working in public services, and street-level bureaucrats in particular, exert an important influence by virtue of their behaviour and attitudes when delivering public services. To understand the impact that the person who delivers the service has, it is essential to consider the role of those delivering a service, particularly in **soft services** (or person-centred services). Unlike **hard services** (like waste collection), soft services (like interpreting services or social services) are produced in and through the interaction of service provider and user. The service itself is produced when it is delivered. The qualifications and the skills of the person delivering it and the way they treat the user have important implications for the impact of the service and service users' experiences. The service itself is hence closely linked to the person delivering the service, and the person delivering the service has an important impact on shaping the service and its outcomes for users (Sarter and Karamanidou, 2019; see Chapter 8). Consequently, public services are key agents in shaping policies and their outcomes not only by interpreting goals and devising ways to put them into practice but also because in the day-to-day delivery of policies, public services and street-level bureaucrats in particular, oftentimes are the face of that policy.

Having explored the importance of implementation as well as the role public services play in the implementation, the question arises which factors support effective policy implementation. Clarity and unambiguity of policies and support of the policy and its goals during the implementation process have been highlighted as important features. As Sabatier and Mazmanian (1979: 485) highlight, it is also important that the 'relative priority of statutory objectives is not significantly undermined over time by the emergence of conflicting public policies or by changes in relevant the statute's "technical" theory or political policy formulation and support'. Further, to effectively implement a policy, those implementing it need to possess the necessary skills and knowledge of the specific policy as well as the areas that it seeks to tackle. In addition, a key feature of successful policy implementation is that those implementing the policy have the necessary resources (for example, the necessary time, and personal and financial resources). This may include funds to hire new staff with expertise and skills, which are necessary to ensure that a policy can be implemented successfully (see Chapter 4). Given the requirements for successful implementation, it comes as no surprise that oftentimes regulation and implementation diverge, leading to implementation gaps (Hill and Hupe, 2002; Hupe and Hill, 2016). This is particularly obvious in the field of environmental policy, where implementation gaps (for instance missed climate goals, such as targets for reducing emissions, which have been adopted to mitigate climate change) have been evidenced and reported repeatedly and in different countries.

Trends and developments

The last decades have seen important changes and developments, from the growing importance of new actors to the emergence of new issues and the increasing importance of existing topics. In the following, the most important of these developments will be outlined.

Over the past decades, several countries experienced a turn towards ideas of a *small state*, which went along with increasing concerns about public budgets and pressures to restrict public spending and borrowing. Consequently, the public sector and public services saw their available resources reduced and were asked to do more with less. Given the importance that access to the necessary resources has for successful policy implementation, this development has important implications not only for the public sector and public services but also for the implementation of policies. European states in particular have shifted from a **positive state**, with its focus on 'taxing (or borrowing) and spending' (Majone, 1997: 148), towards a **regulatory state**. In contrast to the positive state, which awards major importance to redistribution and macroeconomic stabilisation and where spending is a main instrument, the regulatory state uses rulemaking as a key instrument. In this process, where 'rule making is replacing taxing and spending' (Majone, 1997: 139), independent agencies and commissions are enjoying a growing importance.

Further, shifts in the balance of power between different levels of government are an important development. Regional integration increasingly exerts an impact on policymaking at national and subnational level (see Chapter 3). This is particularly true for the member states of the European Union (EU), who must balance the needs and requirements set by European integration with pre-existing national structures and policy traditions. For the UK, the British exit from the EU (Brexit) sees a shift in policymaking towards the national level. Additionally, states like France and the UK strengthened subnational levels of decision making, commonly known as decentralisation (France) and devolution (UK). Several countries have furthermore experienced the rise of independence movements. In Catalunya/Cataluña, for example, calls for independence from Spain have become increasingly pronounced. Independence referenda were held in such diverse regions as Scotland and Kanaky/Nouvelle Calédonie (New Caledonia) in the South Pacific.

In terms of policy content, over the past few decades, new topics have emerged, which are gaining increased importance on the political agenda. Among the topics are sustainability (see Chapter 7), equality (see Chapter 8) and environmental considerations (see Chapters 9 and 10), all of which increasingly find entry into public policy agendas.

Summary

Policies are a plan or course of action devised in response to an existing or anticipated issue, concern or problem, set out and followed by an actor or a range of actors. At the beginning of a policy process lies the identification of a problem, which must become part of the agenda before a policy can be formulated, adopted, implemented and evaluated. Depending on the outcome of the evaluation, that is, the assessment whether the policy has fulfilled the goals it set out to promote, a policy can be sustained or terminated or a new policy process starts to alleviate remaining – or newly created – problems. Throughout this policy process, ideas are of crucial importance as they shape the identification of a phenomenon as a problem and influence agenda setting, policy formulation and implementation.

Public policies and public services are bound together in a tight relationship. Public and social policies are among the most influential external forces that shape public services, their goals, delivery and organisation. At the same time, public services are core actors in the implementation of many policies and are crucial for shaping their outcomes. While policies provide a framework, they leave crucial parts to be defined and specified in the implementation. By virtue of their discretion to interpret the policy and specify distinct ways of implementation, public services influence the specific goals followed, the actions taken and the outcomes achieved. Consequently, public services and those working within them, from those devising strategies for the implementation to street-level bureaucrats, are crucial actors for shaping the impact and the outcomes of public policies.

Key points

- Public policies are important factors shaping the goals, organisation and functioning of public services.
- The policy cycle, a conceptual framework of a policy's lifecycle, encompasses a set of stages, including problem identification and recognition, policy formulation and adoption implementation, and evaluation. Depending on the evaluation, policies can be sustained or terminated or a new cycle starts.
- Every policy is embedded in a complex net of policy goals and is part of a wider web of public policies, which may lead to conflicts between different policy goals.

- Public services are important actors in the implementation of public policies.
- By virtue of their involvement in the implementation of public policies, public services, and street-level bureaucrats in particular, shape policy outcomes.

Questions

- Why are public policies important for public services?
- Why are ideas and actors important for policies?
- Why is the implementation of policies a core factor shaping policy outcomes?
- How do street-level bureaucrats shape policy outcomes?

Further reading

Bacchi, C. (2009) *Analysing policy: What's the problem represented to be?*, French Forest: Pearson. *This book presents an approach to understanding policy through the lens of the representation of problems.*

Cairney, P. (2012) *Understanding public policy: Theories and issues*, Basingstoke: Palgrave Macmillan. *This textbook provides an introduction to public policy.*

Head, B. (2022) *Wicked problems in public policy: Understanding and responding to complex challenges*, Cham: Palgrave Macmillan. *This book provides a thorough introduction to wicked problems with particular emphasis on policies.*

Hill, M. and Hupe, P. (2002) *Implementing public policy*, London: SAGE. *This book provides a comprehensive account of the implementation of public policies.*

References

Béland, D. (2005) 'Ideas and social policy: An institutionalist perspective', *Social Policy & Administration*, 39(1): 1–18.

Campbell, J.L. (2002) 'Ideas, politics, and public policy', *Annual Review of Sociology*, 28: 21–38.

Geertz, C. (1973) *The interpretation of cultures: Selected essays*, New York: Basic Books.

Hall, P. (1993) 'Policy paradigms, social learning, and the state: The case of economic policymaking in Britain', *Comparative Politics*, 25(2): 275–296.

Hill, M. and Hupe, P. (2002) *Implementing public policy*, London: SAGE.

Hupe, P.L. and Hill, M.J. (2016) '"And the rest is implementation": Comparing approaches to what happens in policy processes beyond great expectations', *Public Policy and Administration*, 31(2): 103–121.

Inglehart, R. (1990) *Culture shift in advanced industrial society*, Princeton: Princeton University Press.

Kingdon, J.W. (1984) *Agendas, alternatives and public policies*, Boston: Little, Brown and Company.

Lasswell, H. (1956) *The decision process: Seven categories of functional analysis*, College Park: University of Maryland Press.

Lipsky, M. (1980) *Street-level bureaucracy: Dilemmas of the individual in public services*, New York: Russell Sage Foundation.

Majone, G. (1997) 'From the positive to the regulatory state: Causes and consequences of changes in the mode of governance', *Journal of Public Policy*, 17(2): 139–167.

Rittel, H. and Webber, M. (1973) 'Dilemmas in a general theory of planning', *Policy Sciences*, 4(2): 155–169.

Sabatier, P. (1988) 'An advocacy coalition model of policy change and the role of policy-oriented learning therein', *Policy Sciences*, 21(4): 129–168.

Sabatier, P. and Mazmanian, D. (1979) 'The conditions of effective implementation: A guide to accomplishing policy objectives', *Policy Analysis*, 5(4): 481–504.

Sabatier, P. and Mazmanian, D. (1980) 'The implementation of public policy: A framework for analysis', *Policy Studies Journal*, 8(4): 538–560.

Sarter, E.K. and Karamanidou, L. (2019) 'Quality, qualifications, and the market: Procuring interpretation services in the context of the "refugee crisis"', *Social Policy & Administration*, 53(3): 493–507.

Spector, M. and Kitsuse, J.I. (1973) 'Social problems: A re-formulation', *Social Problems*, 21(2): 145–159.

2

Mixed economy

Elizabeth Cookingham Bailey

Chapter objectives

The last three decades have seen an increasing **privatisation** and **contracting out** of the delivery of public services to voluntary and private sector providers. This has led to a mixed economy of public services which draws on the strengths of different sector providers to deliver more efficient and cost-effective services. This chapter seeks to take a long-term historical view of public service delivery to argue that in fact the mixed economy is a much older concept in public services with the state being a relatively recent addition. It also highlights the importance of these different actors in implementing policies through the services they deliver. Examples from sub-areas across the public services highlight these trends and show innovations happening around the world. As the world becomes more globalised and interconnected, the social, economic, environmental and political factors that shape how public services are delivered also require more innovation and partnership to tackle core issues. It is therefore essential to understand the interactions of the different sectors as well as the challenges and opportunities that these bring.

Introduction

As noted in the introduction to this book, public services, defined as services delivered by or on behalf of the government (for example through public funding) and that are designed to meet certain needs or protect rights, can be provided by three different sectors (public, private and voluntary). The **private sector** provides services or goods for a profit. Private sector income is based on purchases by users. The cost of these goods or services is determined by the market for them, which is driven by demand from users and the supply available through providers. The focus in this sector tends to be oriented towards profits and may focus on efficiency in delivery. The **public sector** is where services or goods are provided for no profit. Generally, there is no directly incurred cost for these to the user, as the services and goods are funded publicly. Money from general taxation is distributed to services based on the needs of the population served.

The recent focus in this sector in the Global North is towards equity in delivery. The **voluntary sector** is also where services and goods are generally provided for no profit. Funding can be based on subscriptions by users, donations from individual funders or grants from public and/or private bodies. In any given country, some public services may be provided by one sector while others are provided by one or both of the other sectors (see Introduction). The combination of sectors providing public services constitutes the *mixed economy of welfare* or *welfare pluralism* (Powell, 2019).

Public services are where many policies are implemented (see Chapter 1). This means that public service organisations are important actors in the policy process. Public service organisations will determine how the policy is translated into a programme (see Chapters 4 and 5). The way they interpret the policy in the service they deliver will be determined by the sector they operate in. The implementation of public service policies by private providers may focus on how to deliver it most efficiently and cost-effectively. The implementation by public providers may focus on how to deliver it most equitably, whereas the voluntary sector may focus on individualised or specialist service delivery.

Starting in the 1990s, public administration reforms aimed to improve public services. The most important among these was **New Public Management**, which was introduced in many countries such as the UK (see Chapter 4). It aimed to increase the efficiency and cost-effectiveness of public services by introducing several private sector techniques to better streamline the operation of the public sector. The intention was to encourage more transparency and accountability in the public sector as well as lowering public spending and costs.

One of the core trends is the turn towards a marketisation of public services. One important part of marketisation is **contracting out** of services facilitated by **public procurement** (see Chapter 7). Public services that were provided exclusively by the public sector are now being provided by the private or voluntary sector. This may be done for the whole service or for a part of the service, like catering or cleaning. The way they deliver that service is determined by a contract which sets out how much money will be provided from state funds to the provider for the service. For example, the construction of a new police station might be funded by the state, but the actual building of this new structure is undertaken by a private company. This may be done where there is no internal knowledge in this area, and it is needed for a short time on a project. For example, planning the disposal of various materials for the fire service in an environmentally friendly way. This development is also seen as part of the introduction of new ideas about how the public services should be managed and governed. However, contracting out of services and procurement is not necessarily limited to short-term projects.

There were also efforts to improve the responsiveness of public sector public services to the needs and wants of service users. The introduction of targets and performance indicators was another means (see Chapter 4). These two elements were intended to encourage competition among public services, in a similar way to the private sector. This was also done by using funding as a means of shaping practices (see Chapter 7).

One of the assumptions made by many people who study and research public services is that state-run and funded services are the default and that contracting out is a new negative trend. However, this fails to recognise that entirely state-run public services primarily emerged after the Second World War. There is a long history of private companies providing various kinds of welfare services, which are nowadays often provided as public services. For example, housing schemes provided for workers by big UK companies like Cadbury. There is also a very important and long history of the voluntary sector providing welfare services through religious institutions, workers' organisations and community associations, many of which would now be defined as public services. For example, religious organisations providing education to the general population.

This chapter will outline the variety of providers of public service beyond the state. As the problems public services face are increasingly complex, it is essential to draw on partnerships and learn from best practice. Therefore, it is important to understand the types of partnerships that can be built, and the different roles played by the different sectors (see Chapters 5 and 7). Other providers may have specific knowledge and expertise beyond the more generalist focus of state-based provision. These providers can be complements or supplements to state-based services. It is then also important to understand the variety of different organisations and organisational cultures (see Chapter 4) that might be encountered when working in any given sub-area of the public services.

Emergency public services and mixed provision

Emergency public services are quite unique in terms of mixed provision as many have a long history of relying on volunteers for delivery of services to cover local needs. This section will provide insight into the mixed provision in police, ambulance and fire services. Some insights into the other volunteer-led emergency response services will also be included.

Within the field of policing there are several models that depend on country context. Some are historically localised and volunteer-driven services which are *community oriented* as opposed to more centralised and militaristic models which are *control dominated* (Mawby, 2011). For example, in England and Wales, policing started very locally and was frequently volunteer driven (Button, 2019). In contrast, in continental Europe, policing has been more centralised and militaristic, drawing on the old Roman colonial system (Mawby, 2011). Beyond the formalised policing structures, which were largely professionalised along with other modern welfare state reforms, there are still many community safety initiatives which are a partnership between voluntary networks (for example neighbourhood watches, mothers against drunk driving, societies investigating cruelty to animals) and police forces. This can also be part of a *responsibilisation* policy to engage communities more in crime prevention (Garland, 2001). The

wicked issues (see Chapter 1) that surround public safety are also requiring more and more joined up teams with collaboration across sectors and governments (see Chapter 3). Additionally, to flexibly meet community needs and to improve effectiveness, some countries still rely on volunteer schemes for community support. These may also be referred to as auxiliary police officers. The UK has one of the oldest volunteer schemes based around special constables in England and Wales, while various states in the US have reserve police officers (Wolf and Jones, 2018). In combination with the contracting out of various support services in policing by Anglo-Saxon countries (for example, clamping cars in the UK or administrative office support in the US), this has created the idea of **plural policing** to refer to the mix of entities and individuals protecting public spaces (Crawford et al, 2005). The extent of this mix will be determined by the ideology of those making public service policy for that community, as well as the history of individual regions.

Firefighting is quite unique in that most services around the world not only rely on volunteers to make up the numbers in case of serious incidents but also include several voluntary firefighting organisations. In the first case, these are composite departments that rely on both paid firefighters and volunteers. Wholly voluntary organisations are most common in rural areas, as can be seen in Canada, the US, Germany and Australia, but can also provide key support in urban environments (Degel et al, 2014). In the Australian case, these have proved essential to combat the increasing number of bushfires caused by climate change, but there is also an issue with retention and recruitment (see Box 2.1). Many firefighting services run and delivered by the voluntary sector rely on taxation as well as additional sources of income. State-run firefighting services tend to be under the authority of local or regional governments with some national oversight. In the UK, for example, the history of firefighting is very localised and based around separate associations, like the police. The Second World War led to the 1947 Fire Service Act, where the national fire service set up in the war years was replaced by fire brigades maintained by local governments with national oversight by the Home Office (Murphy and Greenhalgh, 2018).

Box 2.1: Australian Bush Fire Brigades

Volunteer firefighting is essential in rural areas, as is the case with the state of Western Australia, which uses voluntary Bush Fire Brigades. These were essential in tackling the wildfires that swept through Australia at the end of 2019 and start of 2020 (O'Halloran and Davies, 2020). In 2018–2019, there were 15,817 paid staff as compared to 152,798 volunteers (Richards et al, 2020). These local services are essential to rural communities who would otherwise rely on services from the cities in that region, which would lead to lengthy delays in responses (Birch, 2011). However, this reliance on volunteers also makes firefighting services in Australia more vulnerable to external shocks. There is a question of the degree to which volunteering models in rural areas are *sustainable* (O'Halloran and Davies,

> 2020). The ageing population is one of the key threats because older volunteers are stepping down and economic considerations create competing needs for younger volunteers (Davies et al, 2018). Work, family commitments, migration and poor health/age are other threats to retention rates (Birch, 2011). As with most frontline emergency work, burnout is a core issue (Holmes et al, 2019), as is ensuring a diversity of staffing, particularly along gender lines (Birch, 2011).

In several countries, ambulance and paramedic services are frequently housed together with other emergency services like the fire and police services (for example, in the US, Canada and South Africa). Where there is a large enough population, separate state-funded and/or state-run ambulance services are set up in specific cities and regions (for example, New Zealand). In some cases, ambulance services are state-run and are based within the health sector serving local areas (for example, France and the UK). As state-run provision is reduced in the emergency medical services, it is very common to have either private or voluntary sector run ambulance services contracted by local governments or a mix of sector providers, such as the practice in many federate countries (for example, some parts of Germany and Canada). Emergency medical services encompass three distinct forms: those that respond to emergency calls (with or without transport); non-emergency transport without medical treatment; and those providing speciality care transport between facilities. The first, emergency call response, is the primary focus here, and this can be provided by the state, private or third sector. Ambulance and paramedic services are not particularly volunteer based, but there are several voluntary sector organisations with long historical legacies of providing emergency medical support. For example, St John Ambulance is an international association of charities providing training and emergency service support around the world, particularly across the British Commonwealth. The Red Cross is also an international association of charities providing humanitarian aid and emergency medical support around the world.

Finally, there are several search and rescue agencies that provide emergency services on land and at sea. In England and Wales, the mountain rescue provides support for those lost or injured in the wilderness, liaising with other services. Each local organisation is itself a charity, but also part of the International Commission for Alpine Rescue with constituent members around the world. The Royal National Lifeboat Institution is a charity providing rescue services for the UK coastline which coordinates with the public sector run coastguard, part of the UK Government's Maritime and Coastguard Agency. Within the emergency services there are many examples of charities and private organisations working closely with state-run agencies such as the police to support the public. There is also a strong history of voluntarism that runs throughout the emergency services, as can be seen in the fire service and land and sea rescue services. This mix of provider types, and reliance on volunteers, is essential to providing cost-effective emergency services in low population density areas while ensuring that they meet emergent needs in those communities.

Mixed provision of welfare services

Prior to the rise of welfare states, key wellbeing or welfare needs were met primarily by the family or the **informal sector**, the voluntary sector or by using money to purchase services from the private sector. In the case of the voluntary sector, this could be through various mutual aid arrangements in the community, friendly societies or religious institutions. Religious institutions were historically a key provider of education for the general population with private institutions available for the elite in society. Non-religious charitable schools were also set up by benefactors to serve specific sections of the population. For example, the reformist **settlement movement** in the 1880s in the US and the UK (with some spread to Russia), in which middle-class volunteers moved into poor communities to establish settlement houses which provided education and leisure for the local population (Bradley, 2009). During the Industrial Revolution, governments were motivated to introduce some state-based provision to protect the population owing to poor working and living conditions which impacted on economic productivity and/or in response to political pressures, for instance from workers' organisations or labour movements.

The introduction and/or expansion of welfare states in the 20th century after the Second World War led to the most significant increase in the role for publicly funded welfare services. Compulsory state-based education initiatives grew at different rates until the postwar period, at which point many countries offered the state-based education option up to the school leaving age. However, there is still an active role for both the charitable and the private sectors in providing a variety of welfare services around the world. They are also used to provide the population with choices to select the service that best suits their needs. Charitably provided education, for example, is also still an important element in the movement to achieve the United Nations' Sustainable Development Goals around education and ensuring access for all (see Chapters 3 and 7). The voluntary sector also provides an essential function in terms of providing leisure opportunities and community-based youth work initiatives. Additionally, schools run, or set up, by the private sector or the charitable sector, which provide greater user choice in primary and secondary education, are increasing across the world (see Box 2.2); however, the degree to which welfare states are embracing this privatisation is largely dependent on the ideology of decision makers.

> **Box 2.2:** Diversity in education provision
> One key trend for the study of education as a public service is the increasing privatisation of the delivery of education (Verger et al, 2011). This is seen in terms of the involvement of non-governmental actors, both private and voluntary sector, in

the management and funding of schools, as well as in the development of curricular materials (Ball, 2012). This opening up of state-based education to non-state providers started in the 1980s and 1990s. This was ostensibly introduced to improve cost-effectiveness and improve the quality of education students received. There are two ways this has been facilitated. First, voucher programmes were introduced which provide students with the equivalent money that would normally be spent on them in the state system. They can then use this to purchase services from a private provider. Schemes of this nature have been introduced in Chile, Sweden and the US. Second, charter schools are state-funded schools but operated by voluntary or private providers. These are most well known in the US but exist in various forms around the world: Europe (academies and free schools in England, Wales, Sweden and Norway), Oceania (Australia and New Zealand) and South America (with Chile and Columbia being the key examples here). Several nations have subsidised voluntary sector and religious schools that receive state funds.

Public services that relate to health and social care are very different around the world. Health services may deal with the physical, mental or emotional wellbeing of individuals in society while social care services relate to supporting those who have constraints on their ability to care for themselves. Religious and charity-run hospitals existed in most recorded civilisations, which means they rival schools as some of the oldest institutions providing welfare services, which today form part of public services. Military hospitals were an early form of state-run medical care which often existed alongside a variety of different providers, such as voluntary or charity-run hospitals (Mohan and Gorsky, 2001). Now, healthcare services are primarily run through three models: state operated and funded; privately operated and funded; or a blend of these two. Universal healthcare is used to describe either an entirely state-run service or one where some services may be contracted out to private providers. Different countries have a variety of means of allowing citizens to access these services: schemes where eligibility is by legally legitimised residency (for example, the UK, Canada, Australia and Sweden), public insurance-based schemes funded through employment (for example, France, Japan and South Korea), and mandatory public or private insurance-based schemes funded through employment (for example, Germany, the Netherlands and Switzerland). Often, insurance systems that rely on employment encompass public support for, or funding of healthcare for, those who are unemployed, retired or unable to work. There are also a minority of health systems that are almost completely privately run, funded and operated, such as in the US. However, even with the US, public support is available for those who are low-income unemployed, permanently unable to seek work or retired. The models of healthcare, and the consequent role of private providers, used in different countries are again driven by ideology and the way different welfare states are structured.

Social care services are sometimes also state provided and funded, but universal social care is very uncommon. Social care is one of the more diverse areas of public service delivery in terms of the mix of providers, and still draws on informal family support, community and mutual support, and charitable and private provision, as well as state-based schemes. Funding is similarly diverse. There are also a few health-related support services that are provided by the voluntary sector which run alongside state systems. In the UK, for example, there are several charities that provide holistic support for those in a mental health crisis (Newbigging et al, 2020).

While shelter is a basic human need, housing is generally an area where state-run public services have had a more limited role. Housing (if rented) is primarily accessed through the private sector. There are several historical examples of employers providing housing to their employees, including setting up self-contained communities near industrial or agricultural sites. Alongside these charitable benefactors and foundations, which provided housing options particularly in overcrowded urban areas, state-based housing services have also been used to meet increased demand and frequently provided a means of ensuring accommodation for the poorest in society. However, only a handful of countries or regions in the post-Soviet era have a high percentage of social housing. Many countries have introduced programmes over the last 30 years to allow tenants in public housing to purchase their properties. State housing services now frequently focus on providing affordable housing options. Voluntary sector organisations are taking on a greater role in providing housing for marginalised groups (for example refugees and asylum seekers, survivors of domestic violence) who need rehousing or temporary accommodation, to fill gaps left by reduced public and affordable housing stock.

Beyond the areas discussed here there are several other ways that private and voluntary sector organisations complement or supplement state-run public services. Social security, in the form of poverty relief, was driven historically by religious institutions, philanthropy and mutual aid. While much of this was replaced by state-based schemes, there is still an important role for private and voluntary sector organisations in providing additional support to meet the needs of citizens. Food banks and soup kitchens are a common way of supplementing poverty relief which are almost always charitable in nature.

Additionally, private sector organisations often play an important role in **hard services** (for example, water, electric, waste collection) and supporting public services through public works (for example, creation of roads, dams) and utilities. For example, ambulance services require well-maintained roads while healthcare relies on private sector providers to build hospitals and waste collection to remove medical waste. There is also extensive variation around the world in the mix of providers involved in public works (McKinsey Global Institute, 2016). While in relation to utilities, solar-powered pumps and filtration systems are innovations provided by the voluntary sector to address issues in water and electricity supply in the public sector (Wydra et al, 2019). This can be a way that non-state actors can support public works needed for public services and supplement utility services while addressing issues of sustainability (Chapter 7) and driving innovation in energy policy (see Chapters 9 and 10).

There is also an important role for private and voluntary sector providers to help fill gaps in welfare services caused by emergencies. Non-profits have provided various online platforms for education and the distribution of e-books as a way of ensuring the delivery of public services even in a crisis when there are infrastructure gaps (see Box 2.3). Take the example of the 2010 Chilean earthquake when schools were closed, and voluntary sector providers offered services for hard-to-reach groups. These digital innovations are in addition to the essential health and shelter services provided by voluntary sector organisations in disaster situations. The COVID-19 pandemic has also highlighted the important role of voluntary sector actors in supporting new digital innovations to ensure the delivery of key public services (Box 2.3).

Box 2.3: COVID-19 pandemic and the role of non-profit organisations

The COVID-19 pandemic has been a key turning point for public services. It has also highlighted the limits of (state-based) public services alone to tackle a crisis. Across the globe, community-based groups have been essential to providing core mutual aid to the most vulnerable in society. This has meant providing food packages or food banks to support low-income individuals who are unable to work because of social distancing restrictions. Religious organisations have been essential in providing these supports. The crisis has also impacted the ability of students to attend education regularly and several voluntary and private providers of educational materials made a variety of digital resources available for free. This support has been essential as state-based public services struggled to cope with providing enough materials to support at-home learning. State-based education providers also worked closely with technology companies to ensure low-income students had access to technology at home.

In many countries, it may seem like the historical role of voluntary and private sector organisations in delivering welfare services ended after the Second World War. However, this neglects the crucial role of these sectors in supplementing state-run public services and providing holistic support in areas that could not be otherwise covered. Private and voluntary sector providers are also essential components of contracting out of services to increase user choice and reduce service delivery costs. The degree to which a different mix of providers is used largely depends on the history of different welfare states and the ideology of those making decisions about public services. Private and voluntary sector providers have also been key collaborators with state-run services during periods of crisis.

Trends and developments

Public services are increasingly drawing on digital technology. This important emerging trend is supported by a wider range of sectors. It is particularly vital in the context of a global health crisis where many public services have had to shift to online or partial online delivery. Alongside this, there has been a resurgence in social movements seeking to address systematic issues triggered by recent events around the globe, such as racism (for example, the US, the UK). As a result, public services are looking for new ways to engage with communities to effectively address their needs. The desire for innovation and more connection at the local level is also driving corporate social responsibility work. Corporations are showing greater accountability for their impact across a range of sustainability metrics (see Chapter 7) and taking more responsibility for societal issues. The role of voluntary sector public service providers is even more important, as they tend to have direct access to the communities in which they are based.

This does, however, depend on the way governance of public services works and on the core values of organisations (Bano, 2019). From the state governance angle, managing relationships effectively is crucial. This requires understanding the resources of the different stakeholders, such as their relationship with a given community and their social capital, as well as the goals tied to their mission. It may involve a mix of encouraging competition between different possible services and/or encouraging collaboration (Nwankwo and Richardson, 1996).

For leaders of voluntary sector organisations, building stronger relationships with public services has benefits and challenges. It allows them to influence the delivery of public services by using their established expertise to target work at those most in need. It also helps voluntary sector organisations to identify gaps in public service knowledge about a particular group and provide tailored training. Additionally, service delivery can help to diversify funding sources for these organisations. However, there is also an important challenge for voluntary sector organisations in ensuring that their core mission is not compromised or shifted by these new service delivery opportunities (Buckingham, 2009). For example, organisations that play key roles in doing advocacy work for various communities may feel pressure to reduce activities in an area that might be seen as critical of the state if those same organisations are delivering services on behalf of the state. This is an area of concern for those studying public services, as much of this advocacy work highlights issues, particularly among vulnerable groups, in accessing key public services (Cookingham Bailey, 2021) and the impact of those services on those groups (see Chapter 8). Advocacy work also provides a platform for groups to share their lived experience. This advocacy work is crucial at a time when gaps in services relating to health and education, particularly for migrants and minority ethnic groups, need to be identified if the interlinked issues mentioned at the start of this section are to be tackled effectively.

Therefore, it is important for those working in or studying public services to consider the benefits and challenges of partnerships with voluntary sector organisations. These organisations allow deeper connections to communities, but it is important to also protect the independence of those organisations to maintain the trust of the same communities. Private sector providers can be used to develop innovation to tackle more complex social, economic and environmental issues, but it is important to remember that there may also be trade-offs (see Chapter 7) with the profit motive of this sector.

Summary

In modern terms, public services are thought of as services provided by or on behalf of the state by a variety of sectors. These sectors are the public, private and voluntary sectors. However, when a historical approach is taken, it is easy to see that the balance between sectors providing those services has shifted quite a lot. There is also considerable variation between countries depending on their histories and ideologies. Many emergency services around the world have a rich volunteer- and community-based history, but there is also an important role for public provision in the professionalisation of these services. Whereas historically welfare services were heavily based on charity and mutual aid, in most countries of the Global North, core welfare functions became the purview of public providers following the Second World War. However, over the last 30 years many countries are experimenting with bringing back a greater range of providers into the delivery of core welfare services.

The degree to which private and voluntary sector providers are involved in the delivery of these services is partially driven by ideology but also based on the specific areas where private and voluntary organisations can provide expertise and capabilities that can supplement or complement state-based services. Voluntary sector services have the flexibility and holistic approach that the public sector cannot provide, whereas the private sector provides speed in scaling up services and innovation. To tackle more complex challenges provided by the modern world, those setting public service policy will likely draw on a combination of the different strengths of all three sectors.

Key points

- There are three different traditions that deliver public services: the public sector, the private sector or the market, and the voluntary sector.
- Many emergency services have private or voluntary sector origins and a crucial tradition of voluntarism and community-oriented services that underlies them.
- Core welfare services are frequently provided by the state, but with more complex needs being addressed by the voluntary and private sectors.
- The mix of provision of core welfare services also varies extensively between different countries, largely driven by history and ideology.

- Partnerships across sectors are a means to drive innovation and to access a variety of groups, which is essential as the challenges faced by public services are getting ever more complex.

Questions

- How does the mix of providers vary between different sub-areas of public services?
- What are the challenges and opportunities for those managing public services when working across sectors?
- Why might innovation in service delivery be driven more by voluntary sector and private providers as opposed to state providers?
- How might the delivery of state-funded services impact on the relationship of voluntary sector providers with the local community?

Further reading

Gill, M. and Mawby, R.I. (1990) *A special constable: A study of the police reserve*, Aldershot: Avebury. *This book supports understanding of the history of voluntarism in policing in the UK as well as providing comparison to similar schemes internationally.*

Harris, B. (2010) 'Voluntary action and the state in historical perspective', *Voluntary Sector Review*, 1(1): 25–40. *This article provides a key historical understanding of the changing nature of the partnership between the voluntary sector and the public sector in the UK from the 19th century onwards.*

Roberts, A., Nimegeer, A., Farmer, J. and Heaney, D.J. (2014) 'The experience of community first responders in co-producing rural health care: In the liminal gap between citizen and professional', *BMC Health Services Research*, 14(1): 460. https://doi.org/10.1186/1472-6963-14-460. *This article looks at the complex role of voluntary responders in rural areas in terms of their essential function as medical practitioners who are also embedded in the communities they serve. This highlights the important function of voluntary support in the emergency services but also provides key insight into the experience of individuals engaged in this type of voluntarism.*

Rogers, C. (2017) *Plural policing: Theory and practice*, Bristol: Policy Press. *This text provides a clear overview of how and why multiple providers have been introduced into policing in England and Wales with key international examples.*

References

Ball, S. (2012) *Global education inc.: New policy networks and the neoliberal imaginary*, Abingdon and New York: Routledge.

Bano, M. (2019) 'Partnerships and the good-governance agenda: Improving service delivery through state-NGO collaborations', *Voluntas*, 30(6): 1270–1283.

Birch, A. (2011) *Recruiting and retaining volunteer firefighters in Australasia: An integrative summary of research (synopsis). Report No. D.2:2011,* Melbourne: Bushfire Cooperative Research Centre.

Bradley, K. (2009) *Poverty, philanthropy and the state: Charities and the working classes in London, 1918–79,* Manchester: Manchester University Press.

Buckingham, H. (2009) 'Competition and contracts in the voluntary sector: Exploring the implications for homelessness service providers in Southampton', *Policy and Politics,* 37(2): 235–254.

Button, M. (2019) *Private policing* (2nd edn), Abingdon: Routledge.

Cookingham Bailey, E. (2021) 'Advocacy and service delivery in the voluntary sector: Exploring the history of voluntary sector activities for new minority and migrant groups in east London, 1970s–1990s', *Voluntas,* 32(6): 1408–1418.

Crawford, A., Lister, S., Blackburn, S. and Burnett, J. (2005) *Plural policing: The mixed economy of visible patrols in England and Wales,* Bristol: Policy Press.

Davies, A., Lockstone-Binney, L. and Holmes, K. (2018) 'Who are the future volunteers in rural places? Understanding demographic and background characteristics of non-retired rural volunteers, why they volunteer and their future migration intentions', *Journal of Rural Studies,* 60: 167–175.

Degel, D., Wiesche, L., Rachuba, S. and Werners, B. (2014) 'Reorganizing an existing volunteer fire station network in Germany', *Socio-Economic Planning Sciences,* 48(2): 149–157.

Garland, D. (2001) *The culture of control,* Oxford: Oxford University Press.

Holmes, K., Davies, A., Lockstone-Binney, L., O'Halloran, M. and Ong, F. (2019) *The social and economic sustainability of WA's Rural Volunteer Workforce. BCEC Research Report No. 22/19,* Bentley, Western Australia: Bankwest Curtin Economics Centre.

Mawby, R.I. (2011) 'Models of policing', in Newburn, T. (ed.), *Handbook of policing* (2nd edn), Abingdon: Taylor & Francis, pp 17–46.

McKinsey Global Institute (2016) *Bridging global infrastructure gaps,* McKinsey Global Institute. [online] Available at: https://www.mckinsey.com/capabilit ies/operations/our-insights/bridging-global-infrastructure-gaps [Accessed 25 September 2022].

Mohan, J. and Gorsky, M. (2001) *Don't look back? Voluntary and charitable finance of hospitals in Britain, past and present,* London: Office of Health Economics and Association of Chartered Certified Accounts.

Murphy, P. and Greenhalgh, K. (2018) 'Introduction', in Murphy, P. and Greenhalgh, K. (eds), *Fire and rescue services: Leadership and management perspectives,* Cham: Springer, pp 1–8.

Newbigging, K., Rees, J., Ince, R., Mohan, J., Joseph, D., Ashman, M., Nodren, B., Dare, C., Bourke, S. and Costello, B. (2020) 'The contribution of the voluntary sector to mental health crisis care: A mixed methods study', *Health Services and Delivery Research,* 8(29). https://www.journalslibrary.nihr.ac.uk/ hsdr/hsdr08290#/abstract

Nwankwo, S. and Richardson, B. (1996) 'Organizational leaders as political strategists: A stakeholder management perspective', *Management Decision*, 34(10): 43–49.

O'Halloran, M. and Davies, A. (2020) 'A shared risk: Volunteer shortages in Australia's rural bushfire brigades', *Australian Geographer*, 51(4): 421–435.

Powell, M. (2019) *Understanding the mixed economy of welfare*, Bristol: Policy Press.

Richards, L., Brew, N. and Smith, L. (2020) *2019–20 Australian bushfires – frequently asked questions: A quick guide*, Research Paper Series, 2019–20, Parliament of Australia, Parliamentary Library.

Verger, A., Fontdevila, C. and Zancajo, A. (2011) *The privatization of education: A political economy of global education reform*, New York and London: Teachers College Press.

Wolf, R. and Jones, C.B. (2018) *Volunteer police, choosing to serve: Exploring, comparing, and assessing volunteer policing in the United States and the United Kingdom*, New York: Routledge.

Wydra, K., Becker, P. and Aulich, H.A. (2019) 'Sustainable solutions for solar energy driven drinking water supply for rural settings in sub-Saharan Africa: A case study of Nigeria', *Journal of Photonics for Energy*, 9(4): 043106.

3

Public services and the law

Simon Read

Chapter objectives

The law exerts a major influence on public services. When examining the law in relation to public services, it needs to be considered in a synergistic approach, considering global, national and regional perspectives. With a focus on global influences, it is necessary to scrutinise the role of the United Nations and key legal elements of the UN Charter, as well as the specific role of the UN Security Council and the role of the International Criminal Court in the fields of genocide, war crimes, crimes against humanity and crimes of aggression. The World Trade Organization is important for fostering the development of free trade on a global scale. The function of the European Union and the European Court of Justice also shape the relations between states, highlighting some notable decisions and the operational role of these organisations. On a more local level, and with particular focus on the example of the UK, this chapter examines the role of the devolved administrations' legal framework, highlighting how acts have enabled the administrations to develop a legal framework at a regional level. It will also consider the importance and role of delegated legislation with a focus on statutory instruments, byelaws and orders in council in England and Wales.

Introduction

The law is a major influence on public services. It provides a regulatory and governance framework within which public services operate and sets principles public services must uphold. The role and the interaction of different sources of legislation on an international scale add to the understanding of the geopolitical arena. This chapter explores the importance and the impact of law on public services, highlighting the multilevel nature of today's legal framework. It examines key law-making entities at the supranational, national, regional and local levels, and highlights how legal principles feed down from higher levels, influencing policymaking and legislative reform at each of the lower levels. Examples for this process include a framework outlining privileges granted to citizens by law and protecting human rights, which affect each individual and form a code of conduct in public life but also areas for potential liability.

The chapter also looks at the importance of several international legal bodies including the International Court of Justice (ICJ) and the International Criminal Court (ICC). The ICJ highlights crucial and important developments in the international arena regarding relationships between states. Additionally, case study resolutions from the United Nations (UN) Security Council and case law from the ICC spotlight global issues of collective responsibility. These international bodies impact and pressure individual states through economic sanctions and regional and local influences to tackle crimes against humanity, genocide and crimes of aggression. The process of highlighting and investigating these potential crimes stems often from a state level, drawing on internal expertise in investigation, enforcement, support and security. This process of investigation then highlights human rights violations and the need for the rule of law. Finally, supranational organisations also shape the agendas of national and regional governments. The UN's Sustainable Development Goals and its environmental and ethical standards are also influencing regional law and policy. They have a substantial influence on working practice within public service bodie, which will be highlighted by the Well-being of Future Generations (WFG) Act 2015. This chapter shows the influence of European Union (EU) law on member states on a variety of issues such as human rights, movement of people, goods and services, and fishery policy.

Supranational institutions and the law

This chapter considers the importance and influence of legal agreements and structures at a supranational level that impact public services. A key form of legal agreement that needs to be considered is **treaties**. These international agreements have an impact on parliamentary sovereignty. A treaty is an agreement between two or more states that is governed by international law, which binds mutual rights and obligations to each state. While agreed at supranational level, the process of agreeing treaties is in general not without national scrutiny. In the UK, for instance, the Constitutional Reform and Governance Act 2010 gives Parliament 21 sitting days to review treaties and challenge them. The minister responsible for the treaty answers to any challenge with a statement which begins the 21 days again. If it is not challenged, or the challenge is addressed, the treaty is ratified. For example, the **withdrawal agreement** separates the UK from the EU and shapes relationships between the two entities. This is an example of a treaty which has re-determined the sovereignty of the UK and the boundaries of law. The EU–UK Trade and Cooperation Agreement (2021) is a free trade agreement that covers the economic and social partnership, including transport, energy and mobility; it provides for zero tariffs and quotas on those goods complying with the relevant rules of origin.

It is also important to understand the role of international law as countries are not based in isolation; they interact, collaborate and may be bound by international agreements. Therefore, understanding the global context of collaborative responsibility is essential. The responsibility to protect (human lives and bodily integrity) embodies a political commitment to end the worst forms of violence and persecution. The UN has, for instance, investigated war crimes committed by a single nation state, and consequently public services within that state like the armed forces. The COVID-19 pandemic has also highlighted the key role of supranational organisations, like the World Health Organization. Many supranational organisations set laws, guidelines and resolutions which shape nation-state action on key collective issues. For example, it is essential to understand international courts as they have an impact on international relations, trade and cooperation. Therefore, the following subsections will outline the types of international bodies that influence the national law of member and/or signatory states, and therefore, public services.

The UN

The UN is a supranational organisation made up of 193 member states with a focus on 'maintaining international peace and security', which includes: the settlement of international disputes; promoting respect for 'equal rights and self-determination'; and encouraging international cooperation on key issues (for example, economic, social, cultural, humanitarian) (United Nations, 1945: Article 1). The legal authority for the UN to act on these issues derives from several articles in the charter. Article 2, for instance, promotes the prohibition of force by member states in conflicts and requires them to settle these peacefully.

The UN has six key branches for decision making. The General Assembly is the full representative body for all members. It is the deliberative body of the UN where any global issues or issues between states are discussed. The UN Security Council and the UN Economic and Social Council are two of those branches that issue resolutions relevant to public services. The Security Council consists of 15 countries with five permanent members who have the power to veto any resolution (Russia, the US, the UK, China and France) and ten elected non-permanent members (United Nations, 1945: Article 23). Its focus is on the fields of security and peacekeeping (United Nations, 1945: Article 24). The Security Council has the power to ensure security and peacekeeping by carrying out investigations, authorising military force and arranging peaceful settlements of disputes (United Nations, 1945: Chapter VI). Box 3.1 defines what resolutions are, showcases different types of resolutions that are issued by the UN, and outlines some examples that provide context for those interested in the study of public services.

The Economic and Social Council consists of 54 members and coordinates economic and social issues between member states (United Nations, 1945: Chapter X). The Economic and Social Council's work focuses on sustainable development work and coordinates innovation around the economic, social and environmental dimensions (see Chapter 7). A range of UN agencies work in specific fields of activity and may influence or provide public services. The tripartite International Labour Organization, for instance, works in the field of labour and employment and sets minimum standards in this field. Its conventions may affect the work of public services. The Labour Clauses (Public Contracts) Convention (CO 94), for instance, sets standards for purchasing by public bodies in signatory states and may thereby affect public services (see Chapter 7). Further agencies work in such diverse fields as education (United Nations Educational, Scientific and Cultural Organization), health (World Health Organization) or telecommunications (International Telecommunication Union).

Box 3.1: Key United Nations Security Council Resolutions (UNSCR) for public services

Resolutions are a statement on a matter that the UN thinks is of interest and needs commentary or discussion by member states. These can be **binding** or **non-binding**. If a resolution is binding that means a state, or a collective of states, has previously agreed to accept rulings on a particular topic. This is particularly the case where there is a conflict between two states where a decision, or arbitration, is needed. Non-binding resolutions do not need to be accepted by the states they concern but are used to bring political pressure and awareness on something. This may be used where it would not be possible to get a vote or agreement for a binding resolution. The following examples are all binding and show the range of global priorities and types of issues that are dealt with to provide context for those interested in public services:

- UNSCR 699: UN unanimously adopted a weapons inspection in Iraq to inspect, remove or render the weapons harmless.
- UNSCR 1973: Formed the legal bases for military intervention in the 2011 Libyan Civil War and covered military action against Libya led by a North Atlantic Treaty Organization response. It allowed for the establishment of a no-fly zone and use of all means necessary except occupation to protect the civilian population.
- UNSCR 1996: Welcomed the establishment of the Republic of South Sudan as an independent state. It affirmed the UN's strong commitment to its sovereignty, territorial integrity and independence.
- UNSCR 2249: Gave the authorisation of force against Islamic State and called upon member states with the capacity to take all necessary measures in accordance with international law. This meant coordinating the prevention and suppression of terrorist acts and the removal of safe heavens established in parts of Iraq and Syria.
- UNSCR 2331: UN convention on transnational crime, condemning all acts of trafficking. It also recognised the importance of collection of evidence to prosecute responsible individuals.

- UNSCR 2467: Called for a survival-centred approach to conflict related to sexual violence.
- UNCSR 2375: Called for sanctions of North Korea with 30 per cent reduction in oil and textiles exports in relation to alleged nuclear weapon programmes. The resolution included the inspection of cargo and a seizure and disposal of sanctioned shipments. It also called on North Korea to rejoin the nuclear non-proliferation treaty.

Finally, the ICJ is the judicial arm of the UN and the highest international court. Recognising that a state is sovereign and assuming the commitment by the state to apply the decisions of the court, the ICJ decides, in accordance with international law, disputes of a legal nature that are submitted to it by states. It furthermore gives advisory opinions on legal questions at the request of the organisations of the UN (United Nations, 1945: Chapter XIV). The ICJ's decisions are final and binding. The main areas of coverage include the use of armed force, environmental issues, state disputed maritime zones or islands, state violations of treaties, humanitarian law and state responsibilities. As Box 3.2 shows, the ICJ has high importance in dealing with the relationships between states.

Box 3.2: *United Kingdom v Iceland*: International Court of Justice influence over fisheries

In 1972, the United Kingdom instituted proceedings against Iceland owing to a dispute over fisheries jurisdictions. From 1 September 1972, Iceland proposed extending the limits of its exclusive fisheries jurisdiction from 12 to 50 nautical miles. The waters that surround a country are seen to be an extension of their sovereign land and therefore they have the economic right to exploit the defined boundaries of that resource. The ICJ ruled that Iceland should refrain from implementing these new regulations around extending the zone of exclusive fishing rights, and that the annual catch of those vessels in the disputed area should be limited. This meant that no state could prevent another state from fishing 50 nautical miles off their shores. It was also decided they were under mutual obligations to undertake negotiations in good faith for the solution of their difference. This means, because of this decision, two states in dispute should negotiate with each other going forward on similar issues. Although this case was decided several decades ago, the political importance of such decisions is one that continues even to this day. For example, now that the UK has left the EU it is issuing fishing licences on where, how and how much other countries can fish in its waters. Previously, under EU law, the UK did not have complete sovereignty as the EU law superseded it, but there has been a tiered reduction in access rights since the UK left the EU.

World Trade Organization

The World Trade Organization (WTO) is another key organisation in setting out economic agreements and rules of trade between nations. These agreements have the goal to ensure that trade flows as smoothly and freely as possible. They are the responsibility of the Council for Trade in Goods, which is made up of representatives from all 164 WTO member countries. The Goods Council has ten committees dealing with specific subjects, such as agriculture, market access, subsidies and anti-dumping measures.

International Criminal Court

Under the Rome Statue 2002, adopted by 120 states, the ICC was given its legal authority (Rome Statute, 2002: Article 1). Any signatory state can bring an issue that they want to see investigated to the court. The ICC investigates, and where there is deemed sufficient evidence, tries and sentences individuals charged with crimes of concern on an international basis.

Of major importance for the ICC are issues relating to **genocide**, **war crimes**, **crimes against humanity** and **crimes of aggression**. Genocide is characterised by the specific intent to destroy in whole or in part a national, ethnic, racial or religious group by killing its members (Rome Statute, 2002: Article 6). A recent example of trial for genocide, though not brought before the ICC, was that of Ratko Mladić for crimes committed under his command during the Bosnian War in the 1990s. He was charged over mass murder of the Bosniak population in the town of Srebrenica and ethnic cleansing of Bosniak and Bosnia Croatian populations throughout Bosnia and Herzegovina. He was acquitted of the latter.

The ICC also deals with war crimes, including: the use of child soldiers; the killing or torture of persons such as civilians or prisoners of war; intentionally directing attacks against hospitals, historic monuments or buildings dedicated to religion or education (Rome Statute, 2002: Article 8). For example, on 5 March 2020, the ICC decided unanimously to authorise the prosecutor to commence an investigation into alleged crimes under its jurisdiction in relation to the situation in Afghanistan. This pertained to the Islamic State and Taliban attacks on civilian populations and persecution of women and girls. It also deals with crimes against humanity committed as part of a large-scale attack against any civilian population, such as murder, rape, imprisonment and deportation (Rome Statute, 2002: Article 7). In 2010, the Rome Statute was amended to include the adoption of the crime of aggression, which can be summarised as a state using armed force against the sovereignty, integrity or independence of another. The crime of aggression includes the planning, preparation and initiation by a person who is in a position to exercise control over the political or military action of a state (Rome Statute, 2002: Article 8 bis). This matters to those who study public services from a moral and ethical standpoint, as well as to understand the common value system in place and the variation in context regarding human rights.

European Union

Succeeding the European Communities, the Treaty of Maastricht 1992 established the EU. The aim of the EU is to *promote economic and social progress* and *protect the rights of citizens*. The EU has a specific system of laws relevant to the 27 member states, consisting of primary and secondary law. **Primary law** consists of the treaties. It is the highest law of the EU, which at the same time forms the foundation of EU law. **Secondary law** stems from the treaties and includes a range of different instruments, most importantly **Regulations** and **Directives**. Regulations apply automatically, wholly as well as uniformly across all member states from the moment they enter into force. In contrast, Directives do not apply automatically or uniformly; they need to be transposed within a certain timeframe into national law by the member states. If a member state does not transpose a Directive into national law before the deadline, the European Commission can start infringement proceedings. Further, Directives set principles and results but afford member states the discretion to choose how to reach these objectives.

The European legal framework can overrule the national law of each member country if there is a conflict between the national law and EU law. The *primacy* of EU law is essential for those studying public services in the EU, given that the legislation it introduces impacts many areas in public life, ranging from data protection and cyber security, intellectual property, energy and the environment to minimum employment conditions, equality and migration.

The European Court of Justice (ECJ) is the highest court in Europe for European (yet not national) law. Its main tasks are to interpret European law and to ensure its uniform application. This includes but is not limited to issuing preliminary rulings, which (based on a request from a national court) present an interpretation or clarification of the interpretation of EU law. In addition to ensuring the application and interpretation of European law, the ECJ is charged with the protection of individual rights, and it is a locus to solve disputes among institutions, the member states and individuals. The ECJ thereby acts in five main capacities. Based on requests from national courts, it issues preliminary rulings on the interpretation of EU law. Further main actions include infringement proceedings against member states for the failure to implement obligations, as well as actions against institutions for abuse of power or the failure to act and actions for damages if an individual suffers a loss for which an institution is responsible (Storey and Turner, 2014: 44–47). Its decisions are binding and cannot be overturned by any other court.

National law: the UK context

It is important within the field of public service to have a good understanding of a variety of tools that can be used to generate new legislation and provision (see Chapter 1) as they impact the work of public services and the stakeholders public services work with. In the following, the UK will be used as an example of how law is made at the national level because the legal framework has shaped Commonwealth countries.

Primary legislation in the UK is made by an **Act of Parliament**, which is a **Bill** that has been approved by both the House of Commons and the House of Lords and has been given Royal Assent by the Monarch. Taken together, Acts of Parliament make up what is known as **statute law** in the UK. **Secondary legislation** is also known as *delegated legislation*; it comes in the form of statutory instruments, orders in council and byelaws (the last will be discussed in the section on local law). Secondary legislation is law created by ministers or other public bodies under powers given to them to modify an Act of Parliament. Statutory instruments are also used to fill in the details of various acts. They will usually provide practical measures that enable the law to be enforced and to operate in daily life. Secondary legislation can be used to set the date that provisions of an act will come into effect as law or to amend existing laws. For example, governments often use secondary legislation to ban new substances in response to new information about their dangers by adding them to a list under the Misuse of Drugs Act 1971.

Under the authority of the Enabling Act 1933, statutory instruments are made by government department ministers in an area of their responsibility; they are drafted by the legal department explaining and outlining the purpose and reason for the change. The commencement order gives the date that the act comes into force. Over 3,000 are made each year and are often used to update fines for offences. Parliament's role in considering a statutory instrument varies depending on what is stated in its parent act. Statutory instruments give guidance and assistance around the nuance of how the law is implemented. In an emergency, statutory instruments can be brought into effect immediately. This emergency procedure is only allowed by a few acts when the government needs to make changes quickly. While statutory instruments can come into force immediately, they are subject to retrospective approval from both houses within a timeframe of 28–40 days. If Parliament does not approve it within that time, it stops being law. An example where such legal power has been used is the COVID-19 pandemic.

Additionally, a further kind of emergency legislation, like an executive order, is the order in council created by the **Privy Council**. The Privy Council is made up of a wide range of leaders of the parties in Parliament, Cabinet ministers, bishops, judges and other selected experts. Privy Council meetings are called from the larger pool of people to advise the Monarch on a particular issue. The council can extend legislation to British Overseas Territories, issue proclamations such as Bank Holidays, grant Royal Charters, and is the final court of appeal for UK overseas territories and any Commonwealth country that has retained an appeal to the King in Council. There are two types of order in council, those made under the **Royal Prerogative** and **Statutory Orders in Council**.

The first type is made under the Royal Prerogative, which means that decisions are made directly by the Monarch and do not need the approval of Parliament. This kind of order in council stands as primary legislation and is usually created in a time of emergency. The Privy Council has scope to decide on foreign affairs (for example, antiterrorism legislation). Orders in council can be used for national emergencies, such as the foot and mouth disease control measures. Another example was the creation of the Energy Act 1976 (Reserve Powers) Order 2000 to address fuel shortages by allowing public service organisations, like the military, to move fuel across the country.

The second type is a Statutory Order in Council, which is secondary legislation to an existing Act of Parliament and will spring from the wording of an act. Many pieces of legislation relating to the devolved nations in the UK are examples of Statutory Orders. The Scotland Act 1998 was the primary legislation in the UK Parliament, but the Scotland Act 1998 (Transfer of Functions to the Scottish Ministers etc.) Order 1999 created the Parliament in Scotland. This type of law was also used to create the National Assembly of Wales under The National Assembly for Wales (Transfer of Functions) Order 1999.

Regional and local law

Beyond supranational and national law, many subnational entities have the power to make their own laws. The legal power invested in these regional and local bodies differs between countries. For example, in federated countries like the US and Germany, the states retain a lot of sovereignty from federal governments, whereas in other countries some powers are devolved to regional governments, such as the territories in Canada or the devolved nations of the UK.

Devolution and UK regional law

Since 1999, the devolved administrations in the UK have limited law creation powers in certain fields, like other state or provincial powers in federated governments. **Devolution** is about the transfer of power by a central government to local or regional administrations. This means that there are distinct legislatures and governments in Scotland, Wales and Northern Ireland, which have powers over a range of policy areas previously controlled by the UK Government. For example, in Scotland, the devolved government controls health, housing, policing, education, the arts and sports, environmental, local government, agriculture and fisheries, tourism, and economic development. These powers were expanded in 2012 to cover the ability to raise and lower income tax and stamp duty and the ability to borrow to a limited degree (£2.2 billion). Additionally, in 2016, Scotland received the ability to control welfare and benefits payments and control over half of value-added tax revenues, employment support and Universal Credit in Scotland. The Wales Act 2017, which devolved further powers over several policy areas in addition to those initially conferred to the Senedd, means that the Senedd can pass laws on any subject unless it is specifically stated to be reserved to the UK Parliament. The National Assembly has a significant degree of legislative independence in economic development. In Wales, health and social services, education, housing, transport, and fire and rescue services are devolved. In Northern Ireland, justice and policing, energy, and employment law are all devolved. In Northern Ireland the term transferred is used instead of devolved.

Each of the three devolution settlements involve varying levels of autonomy and power. Some policy areas are devolved to one legislature but not to others. For example, policing is devolved in Northern Ireland and Scotland but not in Wales. This is due to the underlying history and respective political influences of the four nations of the UK. Devolution, it can be argued, has resulted in more effective and tailored policymaking (MacKinnon, 2013). Policies can be produced and delivered that better account for the needs and priorities of the individual parts of the UK. The Welsh Government, for instance, can deliver agriculture policy that reflects the impact of farming on the Welsh economy, while the Scottish Government can run an education system that responds to the needs of Scottish children. Devolution has also encouraged innovation in policymaking (Birrell, 2009). For example, the Welsh Government introduced the WFG, which has set a new template for public services in the country (see Chapter 7). Having four legislatures in the UK means that administrations can learn from policies delivered in one region and then copy or adapt them if they think they will be effective in another (Birrell, 2009). For example, the Scottish Government's decision to ban smoking in enclosed public spaces led to the other UK countries adopting similar policies (Cairney, 2009). The same happened after the Welsh Government's introduction of charges for plastic bags.

Local law

Byelaws are specific laws for distinct geographical locations set by local authorities and public corporations. Covered by the Local Government Act 1972, they include a wide range of areas including marketplaces, hairdressers and barbers, drinking in public, and dog fouling. Byelaws must be confirmed by the relevant government minister but are enforced by the local authority through the magistrates' court and by use of fines upon successful conviction. They are considered **measures of last resort**, which means they should only be used after a local council has exhausted other options and should apply the principles of proportionality and reasonableness. Byelaws come into force 30 days after the date they are made. The local authority must publicise the fact that a new byelaw has been made at least seven days in advance of the date they come into force with signs placed near the area where the byelaw applies. They are also published in a local newspaper. The notice must state the consultation period, of not less than 28 days, within which the public may inspect the draft byelaws and publish an address to which representations on the byelaws can be made within this period. One of the leading rulings in this field is *Boddingtons* v *British Transport Police* (1998, UKHL 13, 2 AC 143, 2 All ER 203), which confirmed the right of a train corporation to create a byelaw. This is particularly important for those studying public services as this means a byelaw can be created by bodies other than local authorities.

Trends and developments

It is vital to consider developments in some of the key areas discussed in this chapter that may have a substantial impact or influence on public services. One key trend is the influence of international law on national and subnational policy, particularly in terms of highlighting issues of note that need global action. This can be seen particularly in the influence of the UN Sustainable Development Goals on sustainability-related policy and law, which national and subnational laws increasingly reflect (see Chapter 7). The *globally responsible Wales* ethos behind the WFG, for instance, seems to build on, and reflect, many of the UN's global priorities. Over the next couple of years, Wales has the aim to become a globally responsible nation, integrating the UN sustainability goals into law and promoting sustainability in recycling. The Welsh Government also aims to couple environmental goals with tackling disadvantages and accelerating their action on reducing emissions. This will help meet Wales' target of a carbon-neutral public sector by 2030.

It is also important to note the importance of political change on legal frameworks and the impact this has on sovereignty. This can be exemplified by looking at the impact of Brexit. For example, Section 29 of the European Union (Withdrawal Agreement) Act 2020 makes a general modification to all existing domestic law, so far as necessary to comply with the Trade and Cooperation Act. The question of how many provisions of the Brexit deals can be enforced in the UK courts under these general provisions is a grey area. However, it does mean in principle that, if domestic laws or administrative actions breach the agreements, then businesses and individuals can have them disapplied by the UK courts. In addition, in the field of human rights law, neither the EU Charter of Fundamental Rights nor the general principles of EU law, established through ECJ case law, could be used to override domestic law in the UK. This is a break from pre-Brexit precedent in how court decisions were made to interpret human rights law. For example, the definitions and guidance set on human rights law that were previously harmonised with the EU guidance could be reinterpreted by the UK Supreme Court, which has potential impacts for law enforcement and border forces. The UK will incrementally reinterpret the meaning and application of each of the principles.

Summary

When considering law in relation to public services it is necessary to look at a wide range of elements. The balance between the state, economic, political and global goals, and needs for development, should be considered, as well as how these dynamics work on all levels of the rule of law. Moreover, considering the law highlights the spheres of influence and control different political entities have over law at each level. This can be highlighted by the work and role of the UN and some of its key organs of application. It can also be seen in the ICC and its work in the areas of genocide, war crimes, crimes against humanity and the act of aggression, which all highlight its potential influence on the state and guardianship over these areas. Also important is the ICJ and its work with states and trading groups to foster relationships and the development of trade and cooperation agreements and decisions. Additionally, the importance of EU law and its supremacy over member states' domestic law when they enter the union was noted, as was the question of how that same law can be restructured if member states leave the union.

On a national level, it is important to consider delegated legislation, such as the application of statutory instruments, byelaws and the order in council, and how these affect everyday life. Taking the UK as an example, it can also be argued that the impact in legal terms of the devolved administrations has been notable and measurable regarding developing new legislation that has been adopted and is being considered on a larger scale. The influence of the WFG has yet to be fully recognised but will be of paramount importance as a method of addressing key issues and concerns at local level in the fields of sustainable development, while improving the economic, social, environmental and cultural wellbeing of Wales. Therefore, the influence and role of legal frameworks from the local to the global level and development of such are key considerations when looking to understand public services.

Key points

- There are several key organisations that are important to know about to understand the role of law on an international scale: the UN, WTO, EU and ICC.
- Between different states and between states and supranational organisations treaties are important for articulating boundaries of relationships, particularly around trade.
- At the national level, there are a variety of mechanisms that can be used to make law, and using the UK as an example there are statutory instruments, byelaws and orders in council.
- Finally, devolved governments are important to develop and lead on new policy areas.

Questions

- What is the relationship between international and national law?
- What is the difference between secondary and primary law in the EU?
- Thinking about the UK, in what situations might secondary legislation be used to deal with public service issues?
- What does devolution mean and how does it work in the UK?

Further reading

Devolution agreements: https://www.gov.uk/government/publications/devolut ion-memorandum-of-understanding-and-supplementary-agreement *explains the detail of the guidance document that sets out the relationship between the UK Government and the devolved administrations.*

EU legislation: Solanke, I. (2015) *EU law*, Harlow: Pearson. *This is a helpful overview text explaining details of EU case law, institutions and the factors that impact on both.*

Guidance on UK treaties: https://www.gov.uk/guidance/uk-treaties *provides an overview of guidance from the Foreign Commonwealth and Development Office (FCDO) with regard to treaties that the UK has been party to.*

International Court of Justice: https://www.icj-cij.org/ *highlights the latest decisions and pending cases before the court.*

International Criminal Court: https://www.icc-cpi.int/ *gives an overview and insight into the cases and investigations conducted by the court related to genocide, war crimes, crimes against humanity and aggression.*

UK law: https://www.legislation.gov.uk/eu-legislation-and-uk-law *provides access to new and existing UK legislation, including how legislation comes into force.*

UN resolutions and case law: http://unscr.com/ *is a key database of searchable resolutions passed by the United Nations Security Council.* https://uncitral.un.org/ en/case_law *can be used to search interpretations and applications of legal texts specific to the United Nations Commission on International Trade Law.*

References

Birrell, D. (2009) *The impact of devolution on social policy*, Bristol: Policy Press.

Cairney, P. (2009) 'The role of ideas in policy transfer: The case of UK smoking bans since devolution', *Journal of European Public Policy*, 16(3): 471–488.

EU-UK Trade and Cooperation Agreement (2021) available at: https://ec.europa. eu/info/strategy/relations-non-eu-countries/relations-united-kingdom/eu-uk-trade-and-cooperation-agreement_en [accessed 7 November 2022].

House of Lords Judgement of 2 April 1998 on *Boddingtons* v *British Transport Police*, available at: https://publications.parliament.uk/pa/ld199798/ldjudgmt/ jd980402/bodd01.htm [Accessed 25 January 2022].

MacKinnon, D. (2013) 'Devolution, state restructuring and policy divergence in the UK', *The Geographical Journal*, 181(1): 47–56.

Rome Statue of 1st of July 2002 on establishing the International Criminal Court, United Nations, Treaty Series, vol. 2187, No. 38544.

Storey, T. and Turner, C. (2014) *Unlocking EU law*, Oxon: Routledge.

United Nations (1945) *Charter of the United Nations and Statute of the International Court of Justice*, available at: https://www.un.org/en/about-us/un-chartee [Accessed 25 January 2022].

United Nations Security Council Resolution (UNSCR) 699 of 17 June 1991 on Iraq, available at: http://unscr.com/en/resolutions/699 [Accessed 25 January 2022].

United Nations Security Council Resolution (UNSCR) 1973 of 17 March 2011 on The situation in Libya, available at: http://unscr.com/en/resolutions/1973 [Accessed 25 January 2022].

United Nations Security Council Resolution (UNSCR) 1996 of 8 July 2011 on Reports of the Secretary General on the Sudan, available at: http://unscr.com/en/resolutions/1996 [Accessed 25 January 2022].

United Nations Security Council Resolution (UNSCR) 2249 of 20 November 2015 on Threats to international peace and security caused by terrorist acts, available at: http://unscr.com/en/resolutions/2249 [Accessed 25 January 2022].

United Nations Security Council Resolution (UNSCR) 2331 of 20 December 2016 on Maintenance of international peace and security, available at: http://unscr.com/en/resolutions/2331 [Accessed 25 January 2022].

United Nations Security Council Resolution (UNSCR) 2375 of 11 September 2017 on Non-proliferation/Democratic People's Republic of Korea, available at: http://unscr.com/en/resolutions/2375 [Accessed 25 January 2022].

United Nations Security Council Resolution (UNSCR) 2467 of 23 April 2019 on Women and peace and security: Sexual violence in conflict, available at: http://unscr.com/en/resolutions/2467 [Accessed 25 January 2022].

PART II

The internal dynamics of public services

4

Organisations and institutions

Elizabeth Cookingham Bailey

Chapter objectives

This chapter provides an understanding of what public service organisations are and how they work. Public service organisations are independent from entities that make laws and strategies regarding public services and focus on implementation instead. This chapter furthermore explores core theories around organisational dynamics, which influence those working in public service organisations. These are important as they allow managers to understand and lead change. The chapter explores the question of how organisations are structured and the culture that underlies them, while relating back to the ideas that have driven the creation of the organisation and determined its direction. This shows the key role of actors in influencing the implementation of changes in public sector organisations. Since the 1990s, there has been a movement within welfare states to consider the stability of the organisations that deliver public services. This links first to ideas of New Public Management and secondly to emergent ideas around co-production of service and e-governance. The degree to which this has occurred has been partially determined by the paradigms that underlie individual welfare states, as by well as the ideological and political forces at play.

Introduction

Organisations are made up of a collection of rules, norms, practices and structures which govern how they conduct their daily operations and implement policies (see Chapter 1) or strategies (see Chapter 5). The rules, norms, practices and structures that underline public sector and public service organisations differ from those that govern other types of organisations. Public service organisations deal with a variety of push and pull factors, as they rely on public sector funding and must respond to public need. Economic, social and political changes impact the organisation. Consequently, public sector organisations deal with a variety of changes which may impact their operations. Drawing on organisational theory, these changes can be defined in terms of those that are **planned** and those that are **unplanned**. Planned change might result from a policy decision (see

Chapter 1), which needs to be carried out, or implemented, within or by the organisation. Unplanned change normally occurs unexpectedly in response to urgent needs. The way public service organisations cope with change determines how well they can achieve the policy goals set by policymakers. It also determines how responsive these organisations are to the needs of service users.

How flexible public service organisations are in responding to changes depends on how institutionalised various practices have become and how workers in those organisations relate to those practices. It is therefore important to consider different theories around **institutionalism** – the study of the relationship between institutional characteristics, the individuals who work in them and how those institutions change. There are a variety of approaches to the study of institutions which argue that different factors impact on the direction of organisations. These can be distinguished into historical, rational choice and sociological approaches (Hall and Taylor, 1996). The **rational choice** approach focuses on the rules that govern behaviour in an organisation and relies on the idea that people seek their own benefit. Taking this approach to considering change means that new rules will be followed if the benefits are clear to employees. In contrast, those taking a more **sociological** approach will consider the symbols, routines and norms within institutions, which are used by workers to make sense of their situation. Taking this approach means ensuring any change to an organisation is reinforced through regular activities and through communication materials. Finally, the **historical** approach argues that the way institutions were set up and what practices have existed over time determines how staff respond to new issues. As discussed in Chapter 2, there is a lot of variety in the background of public service organisations, which also shapes how they operate (Thelen, 2004).

Implementing change in a public service organisation requires overcoming resistance. Depending on the approach taken, this might mean focusing on the motivation of workers, the activities they engage in or on ingrained ways of doing things. All these factors create *institutional stickiness* which constrains the ability of institutions to change and makes them *path dependent* (Pierson, 2000). One key concept within path dependency is the idea of **critical junctions** at which a course of action, or way of doing things, is altered. Critical junctures constitute moments when various external or internal pressures force change. Then new processes become locked in, creating institutional stickiness around the new ways of operating. This chapter explores the different key types of pressures that can drive change: political, economic and social. It then outlines some of the techniques that managers can use to manage change within public service organisations. Finally, this chapter looks at some of the new challenges facing public service organisations in terms of culture, structure and practices.

External dynamics driving organisational change

Several external political, economic and social factors shape the direction of an organisation; for example, changes in migration policy can restrict the types of public services different groups can access. Some of these external influences may happen gradually, allowing for planned strategic changes in the direction of the organisation, while others may be sudden forcing unplanned change. It is crucial for public service managers and leaders to gain an understanding of these external dynamics to lead organisations through change (see Chapters 5 and 6). The following subsections will explore these factors in more detail while showing how they are interrelated and can compound to force a public service organisation to change.

Political influences

Political factors are crucial in shaping public service organisations (see Chapter 1). The very creation of public service organisations is political (see Introduction). Further, public service organisations are shaped by ideology in the way they are set up in terms of their function and scope (Andrews et al, 2011). Ideology shapes policy goals (see Chapter 1), which in turn determine the focus of the public service organisation (see Chapter 2). Political factors may also be the source of changes to the direction of the organisation; then various checks are needed to ensure public service organisations are working towards and achieving the intended goals set out by policies. This is part of the idea of **accountability** in public services, which means public services are answerable to others and held to account (Mulgan, 2003). This is particularly important when a variety of non-state providers of public services are involved (see Chapters 2 and 7).

Accountability can be thought of in larger moral or philosophical terms around what we owe to each other, or it can be used more mechanistically to make organisations accountable for their actions (Bovens, 2010). For those studying public services, both definitions are helpful. However, the mechanistic view, which can be subject to political change, is particularly important for understanding political influences on organisations. Taken in this sense, it can be argued that accountability mechanisms become more important when trust in public services is lower (Mulgan, 2003). Jarvis (2014) notes a few functions that accountability provides. These include accountability as **democratic** in that it allows the elected to review the unelected and as **assurance** in that it ensures resources allocated to organisations to make a change are in line with laws. Accountability can further be directed towards **learning** what is working and/or **results**, ensuring that an action or service is delivering what it is supposed to. Various accountability mechanisms are put in place to check on change and progress within public service organisations. The new focus on accountability in policing in the US, for example, will shape the direction of various activities in the organisation. If more reporting, or individual incident inquiries, is required every time a police officer discharges a firearm, this accountability mechanism may shift the way individual frontline staff think about using their firearms.

Targets are externally set goals which measure specific results and provide a way of monitoring the performance of both individuals and the organisation (Bevan and Hood, 2006). They are an accountability mechanism which provides rewards and sanctions to improve performance (see Box 4.1). As noted in Chapter 1, policies rely on frontline service workers and professionals to be implemented. The degree to which those implementing policies have autonomy in how they make changes in the organisation has much to do with the degree of trust in public service workers. **New Public Management** (NPM) (see Chapter 2) was above all a move away from older models that favoured trust of the public service workers to those that relied on control (Mulgan, 2003; Le Grand, 2007). Le Grand (2013) talks about changing perceptions about public service workers from *knights* with altruistic and public-spirited motivations to *knaves* who only help when it will benefit them in the long term. Targets are frequently discussed to check knavish behaviour by holding professionals to account for their actions. It is important to remember that targets are not inherently objective and rather reflect the priorities of the politicians who set them (see Box 4.1). Therefore, targets can be a subjective way of determining quality of performance in each public service. If a service is seen to be regularly achieving targets it might be seen to be performing well against other services. However, all that can be truly said about the service is how well it achieves the targets, not whether that is improving quality for the service users, for example.

> **Box 4.1:** Targets and ambulance waiting times
>
> One of the early NPM interventions into public services in the UK was the introduction of targets for ambulance waiting times. In the 2000s, the government expressed concern about the length of time individuals were waiting for ambulances. To improve efficiency within the service and to better meet the needs of users, new targets of response within eight minutes for life-threatening emergencies were introduced (Bevan and Hood, 2006). These have since been used as a key measure to assess how well the ambulance service is functioning at any given time. However, there has been controversy over the definition of life-threatening, and also over the issues with setting targets that allow for differences in response times in urban and rural areas owing to longer rural distances and consequent response times (Bevan and Hood, 2006). This showed that the outputs measured by targets were more subjective than intended by the politicians who set them.

Economic influences

NPM has shifted how public service organisations are funded, with increased importance given to basing resources allocated on the degree to which targets are hit by public services. Performance-based funding is also being experimented with in public services, where individuals or organisations are rewarded for achieving targets. This is, for example, the case for municipal government employees in Helsinki (Kotková Stříteská and Sein, 2021) and primary healthcare providers across Organisation for Economic Co-operation and Development and middle-income countries (Cashin et al, 2014). For non-state-run public service organisations, funding arrangements will be based on contracts which stipulate the conditions they must meet as part of that service contract to be paid.

By virtue of primarily receiving government funding, and fundamentally taxation, public sector organisations are subject to economic shifts and changes in political will. The prioritisation of funding is frequently political, but it may also be the result of recessions and other changes to the economy. Separating the economic from the political is therefore challenging. These economic factors lead to resource constraints for the operation of public sector organisations in terms of general budgets and staffing. However, there is extensive variation in how different countries structure, and consequently fund, public services (see Box 4.2).

Box 4.2: Global perspectives on police funding

Looking at police funding around the world shows that the number of police forces as well as the degree of decentralisation is very country-dependent. City, or municipally, run and funded police forces are a particularly North American trend, which means countries like the US, Canada and Mexico will have local, state or provincial, and national police forces. The different levels of police forces will have responsibility for different scopes of criminal justice. The funding for each is then largely based on taxation at the local, state and federal level. Funding is also subsidised by various fees from the public for violation of the law. In contrast, England and Wales have several regional forces with standards set by central government. Control over several public services is devolved to individual nations in the UK, but police funding in Wales and England is not handled by the individual nations but rather by central government (see Chapter 3). Regional forces therefore receive central government funding and local police precepts are also set up as part of council tax to provide local revenue. As the result of financial constraints, and changing political viewpoints about their function, the funding is changing for various police forces. Some countries are redirecting funding previously allocated from the police to other public services to concentrate on more preventative programmes. Sweden introduced mental health ambulances as the first point of call for those with severe issues, which replaces a role previously performed by the police.

As funding in public services is politically determined, there are several competing ideological viewpoints that impact on how these organisations allocate their resources. Two competing viewpoints around economic policy relate to **efficiency** and **equity** (Barr, 2020). On the one hand, governments want public services to use resources efficiently – using limited resources in the best possible way to achieve the desired programme goals. On the other hand, public services need to ensure those resources are used equitably – ensuring limited resources are distributed fairly. This trade-off between efficiency and equity will be most true in public service organisations that focus primarily on the delivery of core welfare functions like social security, education or health. The question then is how public sector organisations ensure equity in the services they deliver while also focusing on efficiency, which is core to both working within funding constraints and potentially ensuring accountability. As Barr (2020) suggests, it is important to consider the original policy aims and then the best mechanisms to achieve them (see Chapter 1). Both those allocating funding to public sector organisations and those leading public sector organisations need to consider the way resources are distributed to different programmes to ensure the aims can be met.

Social influences

A final key external influence on the direction of public service organisations links to the way the populations they serve change and whether and how existing needs change and/or new needs emerge (see Introduction). There are limited resources available for public services, therefore the funding made available to them is often based around the population they serve. For example, in general the number of schools and their size has to do with the number of pupils needing school places. This is partially driven by the deamands of the population for that organisation (for example, the number who need that service) and on the organisation (for example, more complexity of health needs requires a greater range of health services).

Migration has been a constant push and pull factor for modern public service organisations. Since the Industrial Revolution, there has been a movement from more rural to urban populations globally. However, urban populations tend to be more fluid while rural areas might be more stable but smaller. Globalisation has also meant easier international movement of people. Public service organisations frequently must attempt to adapt to different numbers and demographics in a local area. For example, many people moving out of a specific area may threaten the viability and stability of the service, both in terms of who it serves and in terms of who it employs. In contrast, some areas have individuals moving in, which raises demands for public services but also provides a wider potential recruitment pool.

Another major factor is that most countries in the Global North see life expectancy rates (that is, how long a person will live) increasing while fertility rates (that is, how many children are born per woman) are decreasing, a phenomenon labelled as ageing populations. Services and public service organisations will need to adjust to accommodate differing needs, for example by reducing childcare, school places and youth services while increasing social care and related health services (see Box 4.3). However, the impact of ageing populations exceeds funding and resource questions. It also implies revisiting the way in which services are delivered and accounting for specific issues that may relate to older age, for instance a higher prevalence of hearing loss or a decrease of mobility (see Chapter 8).

All these external factors – social, economic and political – shape the direction of public service organisations, as they are reliant on political decisions and public

> **Box 4.3:** Demographic change in Japan
>
> Japan is defined as a *super-aged society* with a predicted one-third of its population over the age of 65 by 2036. The population is living longer while the birth rate is dropping, with a fertility rate of 1.36 in 2020. This has implications for the direction of services as well as for funding in the form of taxes from the working-age population. First, the number of people over age 65 in the workforce has been increasing and will need to continue to do so as pension schemes will be under pressure from the ageing population and the reduction in younger people paying in. Second, this will impact on education services as fewer young people will need school places. Third, this leads to questions about how health and social care services will cope with this ageing population. Japan is also a society that has traditionally strongly relied on informal care by the family, which will be threatened by the reduction in the working-age population able to do the caring and an increase in older people who need to be cared for.

funding to effectively meet the ever-changing public needs. It is important to consider the practices within public service organisations to explore what factors shape their ability to adapt to these external influences.

Managing internal dynamics of organisational change

External influences help form the organisation, set it on its path, and can be catalysts for changes that can redirect its path. How those external dynamics influence the direction of an organisation is also determined by internal dynamics, including how the attitudes, beliefs, values, practices and motivations of the individuals who work in an organisation influence its ability to change. Each public service organisation has a particular **organisational culture** made up of practices and behaviours as well as the beliefs and attitudes that shape those practices (Atkinson, 1990; Blanchard, 2010). The language used in the organisation – for example, the mission statement – is one level of organisational culture, the **artefacts**, or **symbols**, which are the aspects that are visible to outsiders indicating how that organisation operates (Newman, 1994; Schein, 2016). These symbols can even be seen in the way people talk about that organisation; for example, whether it is trustworthy or honest. Some of these artefacts or symbols might be visible in **practices** within the organisation (Newman, 1994), such as how frontline workers in that organisation interact with the public or coordinate with each other. Both the language and the practices that surround a particular public service shape its **values** and **underlying assumptions** over time (Newman, 1994; Schein, 2016). Therefore, external drivers of change (political, social or economic) are met with ingrained practices and values which make it hard for them to change. Managers within a public service organisation must consider both internal and external dynamics when trying to direct change in an organisation.

Techniques to manage change

As noted earlier, external dynamics may result in unplanned change (for example, induced by the COVID-19 pandemic) and planned change (for example, change initiated by policies) for a public service organisation. Unplanned change may make it easier for actors within public service organisations to manage change as it creates a critical juncture allowing change to be implemented. In contrast, planned change may come in the form of policies (see Chapter 1) which require the creation of key strategies within public services to ensure the implementation (see Chapter 5).

From an organisational level, Lewin (1951) provides the most basic model of how planned change is managed within an organisation. It outlines how public service managers and leaders can translate desired changes into actions; for example, how a change in policy goals is implemented in terms of changing day-to-day operations, getting frontline service workers on board with those changes and then normalising them to effectively meet service user needs. Planned change occurs in three clear stages in this model (Lewin, 1951). First, the **unfreezing** stage sees a break from previous behaviours and patterns. Planned change requires managers and leaders to create a *sense of urgency* to break away from the past and the existing organisational culture (Kanter et al, 1992: Kotter and Cohen, 2002). Creating this urgency to unfreeze the practices in the organisation needs effective leadership (see Chapter 6) from those managing the change and implies a strong and well-communicated vision for the direction of the organisation (Kanter et al, 1992; Kotter and Cohen, 2002). The second phase is the **moving** stage where new ideas are tried out to find a new way of working. The moving phase of change involves engaging with groups throughout the organisation. To shift the organisational culture in terms of practices and beliefs, getting *buy-in* from across the organisation is vital. This means that managers need to motivate change with urgency that breaks from the past in a way that members across the organisation agree with (Rose and Lawton, 1999; Fernandez and Rainey, 2006). For change to happen, it is essential that managers and leaders in public service organisations ensure they have clear plans for implementation which allow for the creation of new structures (Kanter et al, 1992). This allows change to become normalised with the creation of a new organisational culture in structures, practices and beliefs. The third and final **refreezing** stage is where the new status quo is introduced with policies and practices that support the new organisational culture. This requires strong reinforcement to *make change stick* (Kanter et al, 1992; Rose and Lawton, 1999; Kotter and Cohen, 2002; Fernandez and Rainey, 2006). Individual actors therefore play a crucial role in implementing policies that require changes to public service organisations. Actors must be politically aware of the influences from outside the organisation as well as the dynamics inside the organisation.

Barriers to change

Several aspects of an organisation can be resistant to change. The organisational culture may be quite challenging to overcome as beliefs and practices have become engrained. Additionally, the structure of more traditional public sector organisations has been described as a barrier to change. Public sector organisations may be rather bureaucratic in structure. According to Weber, bureaucracy is an organisational structure based around division and specialisation (Gerth and Wright Mills, 1948). It relies on hierarchy of authority, where positions are based on qualification and length of service and actions driven by a clear system of rules which are clearly recorded. It is based around **rational–legal authority**, which stems from responsibilities and procedures associated with a position (see Chapter 6). Being more likely to be bureaucratic, public service organisations and public sector organisations have often been depicted as inflexible, wasteful and resistant to change.

Key barriers are not just the organisations themselves, their culture and structure, but also the individuals within the organisation. As already outlined, implementing change that significantly alters the processes within an organisation requires that actors at all levels take an active role. Managers must effectively lead the change; this also means engaging with stakeholders across the organisation and using change management techniques to break through individual resistance. The most important technique is active participation and genuine involvement of members of staff in the change process. This may require extensive education, communication, facilitation and support of individuals in the organisation, which can be time-consuming (Rose and Lawton, 1999). This approach empowers staff to engage with the process of change by learning about it and influencing it. An alternative, or complementary, technique is to use financial incentives, such as performance-based pay, to reward staff members who comply with new processes. In extreme situations, punitive measures can be brought in to punish staff members who fail to comply. However, this will be seen as controlling rather than encouraging behaviour and disempower staff (Rose and Lawton, 1999). Targets may be used to reinforce the change in a public service organisation and ensure that it sticks by relating those targets to the incentives and punitive measures, but again this can be disempowering.

Linking back to the core motivations of public service workers, public service professionals with more knightly motivations will be most likely to engage in change processes that draw on their expertise and their knowledge of the service-user experience. Those with more knavish motivations might be drawn in by the more financial or coercive techniques which may also serve as a means of ensuring accountability. It is therefore important to consider not only the culture and structure of an organisation, which may make change complex, but also the individuals who make up the organisation.

Trends and developments

The following section explores challenges facing public service organisations in terms of culture, structure and practices. Ideas about accountability and concerns about professional motivation have driven changes in the way public sector organisations are managed and organised. This is linked with movements to increase efficiency. The ideas NPM introduced over the last 20 years are an embodiment of this. As a result, the mixed nature of the economy of welfare has grown stronger (see Chapter 2) and providers from different sectors take a more active role as they are seen to deliver things in a different and more efficient way. These developments create challenges to the culture of specific public service organisations and traditional bureaucratic structures which rely on siloed working. Shifting towards more partnerships and collaborations is a way to address dynamically evolving social issues such as ageing populations. At the same time, it leads to more non-hierarchical team-based working, which means changing roles for leaders and managers (see Chapter 6). Public service cultures and structures must adapt to these new ways of working.

Public service organisations are also shifting to integrating more **e-governance** tools and platforms into how they deliver services. This was particularly the case in the COVID-19 pandemic (see Box 4.4). E-governance is the idea of 'public services delivered electronically through a network, either locally or over the internet' (Eliassen and Sitter, 2008: 117). The initial creation of e-governance infrastructure can be quite costly to establish, but once integrated, it provides an opportunity to streamline the efficiency in labour and finances of public services. There are a number of different versions of e-governance that have been brought into public service organisations. One version is with more integrated data on service users, which can be shared between public sector organisations. This is the *government to government* form of e-governance as opposed to the *government to citizen* version which focuses on providing virtual services to citizens (Eliassen and Sitter, 2008). There are key issues in the implementation of the changes in terms of different modes of data capture, partially owing to the different ways that organisations have been set up and the variety of data collection practices that exist within organisations. The static hierarchies of bureaucracies are challenging for a system that ideally should be flexible to respond to the user by sharing data across organisations. There is also a public trust question about the type of data that is being gathered and how it is being used. For example, extensive transparency of data sharing can raise concerns about individual privacy. Key questions in this context are what data do citizens allow public services access to and to what degree can this data be shared between organisations with or without direct citizen permission.

Box 4.4: E-governance and the COVID-19 pandemic
The COVID-19 pandemic has highlighted the technological changes in the way public services work and are organised. The pandemic presented public services with a core

challenge that could be most effectively tackled with an increased coordination between different services. It also changed the way accountability and transparency operated in public services. More frequent data reporting was required for several public services to show how organisations were effectively addressing the challenges. The pandemic also highlighted new socioeconomic inequalities which required programmes of additional support, like providing IT equipment to students, and extended the focus of many public service organisations in an unplanned way. Additionally, many public services were forced to run programmes in new ways which were compliant with public health protocols. Some services were delivered virtually, such as classes in schools and GP consultations, which required key shifts in organisational culture, particularly around daily practices. The shift to more virtual services accelerated a general movement towards more e-governance in public services.

Another form of e-governance is the creation of a virtual one-stop shop which provides the public with all the information about and access to that public service, for instance by providing the platform for booking virtual services. This again raises the issue of various inequalities in access and the **digital divide** that excludes less technology-savvy users from accessing services. E-governance also supports another key movement in the public services, which is **co-production**. Co-production brings in service users with first-hand experience to shape the direction of programmes in public service organisations (see Chapter 8). Service users may be involved to assist with commissioning, designing, delivering or assessing public service programmes. E-governance can provide ways of facilitating user engagement through virtual platforms and consultations. However, it can also pose key challenges for public service organisations which are based on professional expertise, organisational culture and structure. Knavish motivations might prevent professionals from wanting to give up control over different areas, particularly where it may require a change in organisational culture. The rigid and hierarchical structure of traditional public service organisations also provides limited entry points for service user involvement. The benefits and challenges are, therefore, like other forms of partnerships, in the delivery of services.

Summary

Public sector organisations are a combination of norms, rules, the people within them, the practices used to carry out their functions, and their history. These elements become institutionalised over time, which makes them resistant to change. However, public service organisations exist in a dynamic environment of political, economic and social influences, which force change in planned and unplanned ways. To cope with these changes and implement policies effectively, there are important roles for a variety of actors within and outside public service organisations. Public service managers need a strong understanding of the organisational culture, structure and motivations of frontline service workers to bring about change.

This may require using private sector techniques, like performance-related pay or targets, which are part of the NPM approach to public services. Alongside this, managers need to work with a range of external stakeholders, including service users, to implement public service change effectively. Digital tools can help facilitate this collaboration and effective co-production of services, but this too requires overcoming bureaucratic structures and institutionalised ways of working.

Key points

- Organisations that provide public services have certain governing practices and rules, which determine the way they operate and that can be challenging to alter.
- Political influences, largely ideologically driven, can determine the aims of these organisations, the types of accountability processes that are put in place and the way funding is allocated to public services.
- The changing nature of the society in which these public sector organisations operate also shapes the types of needs that they must meet with their services.
- When structures and cultures are set in an organisation, change management tools become essential to enable public service professionals to break from traditional patterns and to tackle the bureaucratic nature of public service organisations in dealing with external change.
- New trends are emerging that are challenging traditional structures in public service organisations with NPM, increased use of digital technologies and e-governance, and co-production with service users and partner organisations.

Questions

- What are the different ways that actors can influence the direction of public service organisations?
- How are new organisational approaches challenging existing public service organisations?
- What key factors do managers need to keep in mind when trying to implement a new policy in a public service organisation?
- How do the different sectors that public services operate in influence the organisational structure and culture?

Further reading

Bolman, L. and Deal, T. (2017) *Reframing organisations* (6th edn), Hoboken: John Wiley and Sons, Inc. *This text covers the nuances of internal organisational dynamics as well as the variety of factors that impact on leadership and management of organisations.*

Handy, C. (1993) *Understanding organisations*, London: Penguin. *This is one of the foundational texts around organisational management and covers the aspects necessary to successfully improve organisations.*

Lawton, A. and Rose, A. (1994) *Organisation and management in the public sector*, London: Pitman. *This provides a key perspective on how organisational issues, and dynamics, differ in a public sector context as opposed to the private sector.*

Mahoney, J. and Thelen, K. (2010) *Explaining institutional change: Ambiguity, agency, and power*, New York: Cambridge University Press. *This book contains key case studies from a variety of settings on the nature of incremental institutional change which can contribute to wider understanding of the application of institutionalism to the study of organisations.*

Pierson, P. (2004) *Politics in time: History, institutions, and social analysis*, Princeton: Princeton University Press. *A text that explains the importance of historical study to understanding institutions. This is helpful for a clear understanding of path dependence, how institutions change, and the variety of factors that influence that process.*

References

Andrews, R., Boyne, G.A., Law, J. and Walker, R.M. (2011) *Strategic management and public service performance*, Basingstoke: Palgrave Macmillan.

Atkinson, P.E. (1990) 'Creating cultural change', *Management Services*, 34(7): 6–10.

Barr, H. (2020) *The economics of the welfare state*, Oxford: Oxford University Press.

Bevan, G. and Hood, C. (2006) 'What's measured is what matters: Targets and gaming in the English public health care system', *Public Administration*, 84(3): 517–538.

Blanchard, K. (2010) *Leading at a higher level*, London: Prentice Hall.

Bovens, M. (2010) 'Two concepts of accountability: Accountability as a virtue and as a mechanism', *West European Politics*, 33(5): 946–967.

Cashin, C., Chi, Y.-L., Smith, P.C., Borowitz, M. and Thomson, S. (eds) (2014) *Paying for performance in health care: Implications for health system performance and accountability*, Maidenhead: Open University Press.

Eliassen, K.A. and Sitter, N. (2008) *Understanding public management and administration*, London: SAGE.

Fernandez, S. and Rainey, H.G. (2006) 'Managing successful organizational change in the public sector', *Public Administration Review*, 66(2): 168–176.

Gerth, H.H. and Wright Mills, C. (eds) (1948) *From Max Weber: Essays in sociology*, Abingdon: Routledge.

Hall, P.A. and Taylor, R.C.R. (1996) 'Political science and the three new institutionalisms', *Political Studies*, 44(5): 936–957.

Jarvis, M. (2014) 'The black box of bureaucracy: Interrogating accountability in the public service', *Australian Journal of Public Administration*, 73(4): 450–466.

Kanter, R.M., Stein, B. and Jick, T.D. (1992) *The challenge of organizational change*, New York: Free Press.

Kotková Stříteská, M. and Sein, Y.Y. (2021) 'Performance driven culture in the public sector: The case of Nordic countries', *Administrative Sciences*, 11(1): 1–12.

Kotter, J.P. and Cohen, D.S. (2002) *The heart of change*, Cambridge, MA: Harvard Business School Press.

Le Grand, J. (2007) *The other invisible hand: Delivering public services through choice and competition*, Princeton: Princeton University Press.

Le Grand, J. (2013) *Motivation, agency, and public policy: Of knights and knaves, pawns and queens*, Oxford: Oxford University Press.

Lewin, K. (1951) *Field theory in social science*, New York: Harper and Brothers.

Mulgan, R. (2003) *Holding power to account: Accountability in modern democracies*, Basingstoke: Palgrave Macmillan.

Newman, J. (1994) 'Beyond the vision: Cultural change in the public sector', *Public Money and Management*, April–June: 59–64.

Pierson, P. (2000) 'Increasing returns, path dependence, and the study of politics', *The American Political Science Review*, 94(2): 251–267.

Rose, A. and Lawton, A. (1999) *Public services management*, London: Prentice Hall.

Schein, E.H. (2016) *Organizational culture and leadership*, Hoboken: John Wiley and Sons.

Thelen, K. (2004) *How institutions evolve: The political economy of skills in Germany, Britain, the United States and Japan*, New York: Cambridge University Press.

5

Strategy and strategic management

Jennifer Law

Chapter objectives

Strategic management is a deliberate attempt to steer an organisation in a particular direction. Many approaches, processes and techniques are associated with it. Strategy, therefore, is about the big picture, about long (or at least longer) term goals and about pulling everybody in the same direction. As a result, strategy often incorporates topics such as managing change, building and selling a vision. This chapter explores the various concepts of strategy and its role in making successful organisations, including understanding how decision makers anticipate the future, engage stakeholders, and look for creative and innovative solutions. The chapter explores the importance of the environment, the strategic choices that organisations can make, and the different types of processes (rational and emergent) that they use. It also identifies the increasing focus on looking to the longer-term future when developing strategies in line with attempts to make public service organisations more sustainable and adaptable.

Introduction

Strategic management has become increasingly important to public services across the globe. Writing about governments, Mulgan said that 'the best have helped their citizens to live longer, safer, richer and freer lives. They have achieved their success by being strategic – knowing where they want to go and how to get there' (2009: 2). Given the importance of *being strategic*, it is necessary to consider in some detail what this means and how (and if) it leads to improved performance.

Strategy is defined by Whittington et al (2020: 5) as the 'long term direction of an organisation'. A strategy is usually focused on the big picture of the organisation and on how the organisation can be successful. It is increasingly recognised that a crucial element of developing an effective strategy is strategic thinking. Typical definitions of this involve elements such as reflection and thinking which is creative, visionary and systematic. **Strategic thinking** often uses insights about the organisation and its external environment to help solve problems with the aim of improving performance. **Strategic planning** is often seen as following on from this process of strategic thinking and tends to be characterised as a formal and rational approach in which there is detailed and careful analysis of issues resulting in clear action plans for implementation. This suggests that there is a linear approach where strategic thinking and strategy formulation take place, followed by implementation. This is, of course, a simplistic distinction and there are many overlaps, both in the ways that the concepts are used in the academic and practitioner literature, and in how these processes operate in the real world.

The practice of **strategic management** is currently widespread in public service organisations, although it originated in the private sector and was based on the quest to ensure that firms could be successful in the marketplace. Academic research has followed practice: although early studies were focused on the private sector, more recently there has been an increase in research that explores strategy in relation to public and voluntary sector organisations (Andrews et al, 2012; Joyce, 2015). Historically much of the literature on the public sector used the term strategic planning rather than strategic management. Strategic planning is a 'deliberate, disciplined effort to produce fundamental decisions and actions that shape and guide what an organization (or other entity) is, what it does, and why' (Bryson et al, 2018: 317). Strategic management is broader than this, incorporating strategic thinking and planning but also examining the implementation of strategies, thus drawing on ideas about the internal culture of the organisation (see Chapter 4) and leadership (see Chapter 6). This chapter therefore draws on existing research that focuses both on strategic planning and on strategic management.

Strategic management as a field of study (and a practice in organisations) is therefore broad, but it is based on the major initiatives that organisations develop and put into practice to be successful. While success in the private sector is comparatively easily measured through indicators such as profit, for public service organisations it can be varied and incorporate outcomes such as reducing homelessness or regenerating a local community. Key aspects of strategic management include the context that organisations operate within (the internal and external environments), what they decide to do (the content of the strategy) and how they make the strategy and put it into practice (strategy processes of formulation and implementation). The chapter explores these strategic management issues of context, content and process, and examines the evidence that strategic management makes a difference to public service performance. It also explores some of the emerging issues impacting on strategic management in the public sector.

Strategic management: context, content and process

There are many reasons why public organisations would try to be strategic and use techniques of strategic management. It may, for example, be because of a genuinely felt belief that it will improve performance and enhance accountability (see Chapter 4). It could, however, also be part of a management *fad, fashion* or professional norms about what they should be doing (Bryson et al, 2018). Professional norms are routine behaviours adopted as a matter of course because they are *expected*; in a workplace, this could include simple things (such as what it is suitable to wear or how to behave in a meeting) as well as more complex issues, such as what managers should do (see Chapter 6). There could also be political reasons for adopting strategic management. Federal agencies in the US, for example, were mandated to engage in strategic planning in the Government Performance and Results Act 1993, producing long-term strategic plans which outlined their mission and performance information to evaluate their results. Whatever the reasons behind the adoption of strategic management, evidence suggests that strategic management is part of normal practice in public services across the world (George et al, 2020). But what does it involve? Whittington et al (2020) suggest that strategic management can be thought of as a framework that includes the strategic position of the organisation, the strategic choices it makes and what they describe as strategy in action. These relate broadly to the context, strategy content and strategic processes discussed in the following subsections.

Strategic context

The strategic position of an organisation or its context includes factors in its internal and external environments that can have an impact on its strategy as well as on the goals or purpose of the organisation (Whittington et al, 2020). The importance of the strategic context is outlined by Ferlie and Ongaro (2015: 121) who argue that it is 'a remarkably significant feature' and that currently little about it is contained in the strategic management literature. Of course, the strategic context can vary significantly between organisations as well as between sectors.

One of the most important elements of the strategic context is the goals of an organisation. Those developing strategies will need to reflect on what the organisation is trying to achieve and what its purpose is. Public service organisations typically have more complex and more ambiguous goals than private organisations and there may also be less agreement over them (see Chapter 2). For example, schools may have several goals that are contested – should they focus on getting pupils to pass exams, to get jobs, or to be emotionally resilient? For other types of organisations their purposes may be narrower and more widely accepted, such as to increase sales or turnover. In some cases, shared goals can be used to encourage organisations to try and work together better. In Wales, the government has identified a set of seven Well-being Goals which are supposed to be overarching and include aims such as *a healthier Wales* and *a more equal Wales* (see Chapter 7). These goals apply to a wide range of organisations, including local government, fire and rescue authorities, national parks and the Welsh Government itself.

Another key aspect of the strategic context is the **external environment**. As was noted in Chapter 4, it is widely accepted that organisations will perform better if they are aware and responsive to changes in their environment. This is true for all types of organisations – public, private and voluntary sector. Private sector organisations will need to be aware and responsive to changes such as those of customer demands to survive. For those delivering public services this market mechanism does not usually operate. In a few cases *customers* of public services may be able to choose a different service if they are unhappy but in most cases this option is not available (see Chapter 2). However, public service organisations may incur service user unhappiness if they do not adapt and change; they may be penalised by regulators or punished by politicians. Understanding the environment and being alert to any changes can also lead to better strategies and ultimately to more effective organisations. Quirk wrote that high performing councils are 'attentive to the dynamically changing needs of their citizens; and they are alert to emerging opportunities in their operating context' (2015: 22). However, even with the best of intentions some organisations and leaders may not be good at scanning the environment. It is usually easier to see stronger signals in the environment, as they are clearer and more observable trends. Weak signals can also be significant, but they are often small and individual pieces of data that are hard to identify. For example, very few organisations picked up on the signals or early warning signs of the collapse of the housing bubble in the US in 2008. The environment matters in other ways too; research has also shown that it is more difficult for some public service organisations to perform well than others because they operate in a more difficult environment (Andrews et al, 2012). Environments that are more complex (in terms of client diversity and dispersion), where lower resources or capacity are available (for example, levels of deprivation) and where the environment changes more rapidly, are associated with lower levels of performance. For example, levels of poverty in a local community will impact on services such as healthcare for a range of reasons, including the ability to buy healthy food and the extent of risky behaviours such as smoking, poor diet, higher alcohol consumption and physical inactivity (King's Fund, 2020).

The analysis of the external environment can feature a wide range of aspects, including the country and the political–administrative culture, stakeholders, and political, legal, environmental and social factors. Several well-known models help organisations think about and assess their environment to take strategic action. One of these is a Political, Economic, Social, Technological, Legal, Environmental (PESTLE) analysis, which is used to analyse factors that apply to all types of organisations, whichever sector they are in. This type of environmental analysis can be undertaken for different departments or sections of an organisation, not just the organisation as a whole. Box 5.1 outlines the different elements of the model in more detail and provides some examples from a PESTLE analysis undertaken by a housing association in the UK, Network Homes, as part of its five-year strategic plan.

Box 5.1: PESTLE analysis of a UK housing association

A housing association in the UK, Network Homes, undertook a PESTLE analysis as part of its five-year strategic plan. The PESTLE analysis included but was not limited to the following considerations:

- Political: Brexit negotiations between the UK Government and the European Union, the impact of the Grenfell Tower tragedy, and the new London Plan and Housing Strategy introduced by the London mayor.
- Economic: interest rates have risen slightly but will remain below the long run average for several years, housing associations will need to strengthen income-generating activity.
- Social: growing inequalities between richer and poorer sections of society (particularly in London) are creating increasing polarisation and risk damaging community cohesion.
- Technological: innovation in building technologies brings the potential to improve construction practices and efficiency; growing need for social housing tenants to have internet access.
- Legal: risks of increased legal action, evictions and costs as residents struggle with welfare cuts and austerity.
- Environmental: momentum will grow towards divestment of fossil fuels and the cost of renewable energy will start to fall.

In their analysis, Network Homes incorporate strong signals such as Brexit but also weaker signals. For example, they outline that 'less tangible, yet illustrated in many different forums, is the sense of a distinct change in public mood. Social, political, and economic discontents have manifested themselves in political votes, in the reaction to Grenfell, and with increasing force through social media. Again, this seems unlikely to change quickly' (Network Homes, 2018: 1). The strategy objectives related to this in their plan include 'communicating better and more consistently with our customers' and 'ensuring the resident voice is influential in the future development of our business' (Network Homes, 2018: 10). The environmental analysis provided them with a framework to consider issues that could affect, either positively or negatively, what they wanted to achieve as a housing association and was used to feed not only into their strategic decisions in relation to issues such as strategy content (what they should do) but also into strategy processes (how they should make and implement strategy).

A key aspect of any organisation's context is its stakeholders. The term stakeholder has typically referred to anyone who *has a stake* in the organisation, and this can incorporate a range of groups such as service users, funders, staff and regulators. There has been a significant shift in the past 20 years to focusing on the *service user*, which has led to changes in the way that strategies are made (the processes).

Public service organisations are now more likely to incorporate service user views into their strategies and to consult them about the way forward (see Chapters 4 and 8). Examples of this include participatory budgeting in Porto Alegre in Brazil where around one-fifth of the local population said they had been involved in the process (World Bank, 2008). Other important stakeholders could be groups such as board members of voluntary sector organisations, as well as any regulatory bodies. Of course, there may be some stakeholders who are more powerful than others and a classic approach to **stakeholder management** has been to consider the relative power of different stakeholders as well as their level of interest in the issues in question (the **stakeholder power matrix**) and to manage them accordingly. Hence, in the stakeholder power model, those stakeholders who are deemed both powerful and interested in a specific issue would be managed differently (keep them satisfied) to those who were neither interested nor powerful (keep them informed).

The internal context relates to the organisation itself and its resources, staffing, capabilities and culture. This is a key element of analysing the strategic context. For example, if an organisation finds that its culture is problematic it may lead to a strategy being developed to address this. Staff may be key stakeholders in some strategies and their attitudes and abilities may also be considered in strategy processes of formulation and implementation. Staff engagement in strategy development is widely accepted as good practice and is important not only for gaining insights from those who have the most direct experience of an issue or service but also for gaining staff understanding and acceptance of the proposed strategy. There may also be strategies developed to try and change aspects of the organisation such as culture and skill sets. A recent example of this in the UK is the Declaration on Government Reform, which seeks to widen the pool of people coming into the civil service, to enhance diversity, to encourage innovation and to improve project management, data, digital and science skills (Cabinet Office, 2021).

Strategy content and strategic choices

Strategy content can be defined as what organisations have done, or the strategic choices they are making currently, or have made over time. Historically, research on strategic management in public organisations tended not to focus on strategy content. It was sometimes assumed that public sector organisations were simply bureaucratic organisations with little freedom because of factors such as legislative constraints and a lack of resources. However, more recently it has been recognised that many public service organisations have autonomy and research has begun to investigate the strategic choices that have been made and the impact that this has had on performance (Andrews et al, 2012).

In the private sector strategic management literature, a significant focus lies on strategy content. This typically focuses on how organisations relate to competitors and how they can compete in a market. This literature incorporates issues such as those that are outlined in Porter's (1980) classic **competitive strategy theory**, such as should an organisation focus on low prices to compete, or on differentiating enough to create products that customers are willing to buy at a higher price? Other considerations in relation to strategy content include questions such as whether the organisation should move into new markets or not. Should it outsource some of the work or keep everything in-house? Should it engage in mergers and acquisitions or not? Another classic model of strategy content is the **Resource Based Theory** (Hamel and Prahalad, 1994) which focuses on the strengths of an organisation as a basis for developing their strategic options. In this model, organisations may be able to gain strategic advantage in a market if they have tangible (for example buildings) and/or intangible (for example knowledge, skills) assets that others do not have. The advantage is enhanced if the resources are valuable, rare, cannot be imitated and cannot easily be substituted. At first glance it is easy to assume that these questions of strategy content or choices do not apply to public service organisations. Often, they are not competing with others for business, do not have the option of moving into new geographical markets, or usually of creating and selling new products. They also often face legal constraints and obligations in terms of service provision (see Chapters 3 and 8) and are not easily able to raise additional funds as they are typically dependent on government budgets.

However, it is important to remember that public service organisations, and even different departments within organisations, vary widely. While some operate routine, rule-based procedures with little scope for variation, others have more flexibility. They may be able to provide new types of services in new ways, and some, such as those in the voluntary sector, may also be able to operate in different geographical locations. Similarly, several public organisations frequently make the decision about whether to provide services directly or to *contract* to the private or voluntary sector (see Chapter 7). Hansen and Ferlie (2014) point out that strategic management models such as that developed by Porter and the Resource Based Theory are more applicable in what they describe as *New Public Management (NPM) rich organisations*. These are organisations such as secondary schools in Denmark and higher education in England that have a high degree of autonomy, performance-based budgets and that operate in market-like conditions. This means that they have more freedom from political oversight and more choices about what strategies to pursue. These organisations also have an incentive to gain more *customers* as this will bring in additional resources. Hansen and Ferlie (2014) also point out that there are other public service organisations which may be at the other end of this continuum and therefore these ideas may have less relevance.

Research also found evidence of different strategic approaches within organisations. Based on service departments of local authorities in Wales, Andrews et al (2012) explored strategy in the public sector using the classic Miles and Snow (1978) classification of strategy (ideal types). Drawing on insights from organisational strategy in the private sector, Andrews et al (2012) explored different strategies in the public sector. They found that some organisations (**prospectors**) are likely to be innovative, a first mover in the field, and more likely to take risks. Others (**defenders**) are more conservative, likely to focus their attention on existing services and to be late adopters of innovations. A third type of organisations (**reactors**) are those that do not have a strategy as such and simply respond to different pressures from the environment. Andrews et al (2012) found all types of strategies, which had previously been identified in the private sector (Miles and Snow, 1978), in operation in departments in Wales. This indicates that strategies of prospecting and defending were associated with higher performance (as measured through effectiveness) and that both strategies outperformed reactors. This study also adds weight to the argument that public service organisations vary and that therefore universal concepts and ideas in relation to strategic management (and other topics) may not be appropriate.

Innovation is a key element of the prospector stance, and it is something that has been strongly encouraged by governments across the world. Innovation does not necessarily mean inventing something completely new. Mulgan identifies public sector innovation as:

> [C]reating, developing and implementing practical ideas that achieve a public benefit. These ideas have to be at least in part new (rather than improvements); they have to be taken up and used (rather than simply remaining ideas); and they have to be useful. By this definition innovation overlaps with, but is different from, creativity and entrepreneurship. (Mulgan, 2014: 5)

Mulgan also points out that while many organisations wait to be prompted to innovate, the best ones are being proactive, looking and scanning the environment to learn and adapt (Mulgan, 2014). The Organisation for Economic Co-operation and Development (2017: 249–250) similarly recognises the need for innovation in the public sector globally and sets out key actions that it considers to be the primary enablers for this, such as enhancing the culture of the civil service, encouraging the free flow of information and data, and ensuring that organisational structures, rules and processes are appropriate. These enablers should enhance innovation and the development of new strategies in a range of ways. For example, action one suggests that organisations need to ensure that incentives and norms encourage innovation. If they do, then staff working in public service organisations will expect to bring forward new and innovative strategies and try new things to achieve the objectives of the organisation.

Strategy processes: formulation and implementation

Strategy processes are the approaches that organisations take when they formulate and implement strategies. They focus on how the strategy is made and how it is put into practice. This links to what the public policy literature calls policy formulation and policy implementation (see Chapter 1). **Strategy formulation** is the study of how strategies are developed. It is an aspect of strategic management that has been studied extensively by scholars in the public management and strategic management fields (Mintzberg et al, 1998) and there are a wide range of models of this, some descriptive and some normative.

Much of the debate about different models of strategy processes centres on whether strategies should be made in a rational or incremental/emergent way. A **rational approach** to strategy formulation involves a formal, analytical process where organisations first scan the environment, then alternative options are assessed, and the *best* chosen to be implemented. There is a long history of this approach to planning in the public sector in many countries. For example, in the UK, corporate planning was introduced to local government in the 1970s and had many of the characteristics of rational planning. However, assessments of this 1970s experience show that it was not effective due to problems such as the technical difficulty of obtaining all the data needed to do a full assessment of the environment and the impact of all alternative strategy options. This approach led to what was described as *paralysis by analysis* and the production of many detailed plans that were never put into practice.

Currently, very few organisations in the public and voluntary sector engage in this very detailed and rigid approach, instead most operate a more *realistic and achievable* model of it. They have a formal and deliberate process which contains many of the elements of a rational approach – goals, evaluation of the external and internal environments, then evaluation of the strategic options followed by more operational plans relating to budgets and to other specific departments. This rational approach to planning is described as ubiquitous in the US, operating in federal departments and agencies, state agencies and some local government jurisdictions (Bryson, 2010).

Critics of the rational approach point to an alternative – **incremental** or **emergent** strategy making. Mintzberg et al (1998) suggest that most strategies are not planned by senior managers as such, but rather *emerge* from the routine practices of staff. They argue that the strategies that are formally planned are rarely implemented (there is therefore an implementation deficit) and they also criticise the rational approach as it assumes a divide between the formulation and the implementation of strategy. The emergent approach builds on the logical incrementalist approach of strategy making which suggests that senior managers may just set out broad goals, and that decision making is a series of political compromises between key actors, rather than a carefully analysed and evaluated option. Hence strategy evolves over time, rather than being planned in advance. The emergent approach clarifies this further, as strategies are often those identified by looking back at a pattern of decisions. Strategy in this case relates more to activities that take place from the *bottom up* rather than being planned from the *top down*.

The effective implementation of strategy is crucial to organisational success, but it has been argued that as many as half of strategies in the public sector are not fully implemented. Strategy implementation involves the communication, adoption and enactment of strategic plans. Andrews et al (2012) explore styles of strategy implementation – the approach that organisations take when putting policies into practice. These can be varied with rational styles at one end of the spectrum and incremental at the other. A more rational approach would have more centralised control and include clearly defined activities through processes such as business plans, which would identify tasks and targets. A more incremental approach would have decentralised responsibility and a much looser distinction between strategy formulation and implementation and a high level of staff involvement in the process.

Strategic management is complex – incorporating context, content and processes – and it can therefore be difficult to provide universal recommendations for organisations. However, it is striking that evidence increasingly indicates that it can improve performance (Bryson, 2010). Andrews et al (2012: 160–161), for instance, found that 'all three of the major elements of strategic management matter for the effectiveness of public services: 1. Strategy content, 2. Formulation and 3. Implementation'. Significantly, they found that contingencies between these aspects were important, leading them to highlight that 'the links between strategy and performance are complex and varied, not simple and uniform, and it is conceivable that different strategies will be equally effective, depending on the internal and external circumstances of the organisation' (Andrews et al, 2012: 161).

Trends and developments

In 2010, in a special issue of *Public Administration Review* which looked forward to the next ten years, several academics argued that strategic management would become more important as public services tried to both anticipate and manage change and cope with new issues as they rapidly emerged. Writing after the 2005 Hurricane Katrina disaster in the US, McGuire and Schneck (2010: 201) argued that strategic management capacity was crucial and 'successful emergency preparedness, response, and recovery in the future are largely functions of the degree to which government leaders possess strategic management capacity'. In 2021, the world was in the middle of the global emergency caused by COVID-19. Most countries used some strategic management techniques to try and deal with this crisis but also to prepare better for the future. One of these is scenario planning, where different possible or probable futures are used to inform thinking and strategic planning. The Monitor Institute, for example, offers four scenarios for the voluntary sector to consider when planning for the future, titled *a return to normal*; *a rise from the ashes*; *social fabric unravelled*; and *a nation on the brink* (Kasper et al, 2020: 11). Other approaches to envision the future are also encouraged by governments; the UK Government has published a toolkit for policymaking professionals on foresight and the different techniques that can be used to support futures thinking (Cabinet Office, 2014). More broadly, many organisations are seeking to think strategically and lengthen the timeframe for their strategic plans. Of course, this creates challenges as there is more uncertainty over the future.

Information, data and insight are needed to inform this type of strategic management, perhaps more so now, as the environment is more uncertain. When the environment is relatively stable, strategic management is more straightforward, but as the context shifts and becomes less stable, strategic management becomes more difficult. One of the challenges for strategic management is to be alert to changes in the environment and to pick up these signals (both strong and weak signals). There is increasing data available to strategic managers. This includes data such as national level censuses, which in the UK, for example, take place every ten years. NPM type public service reform in many countries over the past 30 years means that public service organisations are now well informed about their customers, service users or residents and are therefore able to use this information to try and improve their services. In addition, data from sources such as social media is increasingly available. Used well, this *big data* can enhance strategy making as it provides better understanding, but there is also a danger that so much data may make it hard to see some of the signals.

Another trend is that public service organisations in many countries are increasingly working with partners to achieve their objectives. This offers many benefits but requires different approaches to strategic management. Working in a more collaborative and networked way means that public service organisations will find it more difficult to impose *top-down* strategies. Instead of relying on rational planning skills, Klijn and Koppenjan (2020) suggest that organisations will rely more on leadership skills such as motivation, negotiation and conflict management.

Summary

Public service organisations across the globe are increasingly using strategic management approaches and techniques. In part, this is because there is evidence that this can help them to achieve their objectives. Public service organisations are also refining and adapting these approaches and techniques so that they fit their changing needs more effectively. As organisations change the way that they operate, to be, for example, more inclusive (see Chapter 8), to focus more on sustainability (see Chapter 7) and reduce their environmental impact (Chapters 9 and 10), and to increasingly work with others, there is a need to reflect this in the way that they *do strategic management*. There are, of course, many ways to assess the strategic context, different strategic choices that can be made, and approaches to strategy processes that range from rational to emergent. Research has shown that there is not one specific approach that will be right for all organisations, in all situations.

Key points

- The environment for public service organisations is complex and rapidly changing and a crucial element of strategic management is being aware of this and adapting services as needed.
- Effective strategic planning requires understanding the internal and external environments (context), the choices that organisations can make (the content) and the processes (rational and emergent) available to them.
- There is no one universal *best way* to undertake strategic management which will work for all organisations in all circumstances.
- Many public service organisations are part of a network of organisations working to achieve specific outcomes, and strategic management in this context may require different skills and capabilities.

Questions

- Think of three public service organisations that have a lot of autonomy and three that have very little. What are the factors that give them autonomy and why might this be important for strategic management?
- Why might a rational approach to strategy formulation and implementation be useful?
- What are the advantages of a more incremental or emergent approach to strategy formulation and implementation?
- What do you think are the most important emerging trends in strategic management?

Further reading

Clegg, S.R., Schweitzer, J., Whittle, A. and Pitelis, C. (2019) *Strategy: Theory and practice*, London: SAGE. *This textbook provides an excellent introduction to the field of strategic management and covers topics such as strategy as practice and organisational politics which are not always covered in other texts.*

Grant, R. (2021) *Contemporary strategy analysis*, Chichester: Wiley. *This textbook focuses on strategic analysis, examining both the organisation and the environment that it operates within. It incorporates up-to-date issues such as the impact of COVID-19 and environmental, social and governance innovations.*

References

Andrews, R., Boyne, G., Law, J. and Walker, R. (2012) *Strategic management and public service performance*, Basingstoke: Macmillan.

Bryson, J. (2010) 'The future of public and nonprofit strategic planning in the United States', *Public Administration Review*, 70(1): 255–267.

Bryson, J., Edwards, L.H. and Van Slyke, D. (2018) 'Getting strategic about strategic planning research', *Public Management Review*, 20(3): 317–339.

Cabinet Office and Government Office for Science (2014) Guidance of 8 July 2014 on Futures Toolkit: Tools for policy-makers and analysts, available at: https://www.gov.uk/government/publications/futures-toolkit-for-policy-makers-and-analysts [Accessed 25 January 2022].

Cabinet Office (2021) Declaration of 15 June 2021 on government reform, available at: https://www.gov.uk/government/publications/declaration-on-government-reform [Accessed 25 January 2022].

Ferlie, E. and Ongaro, E. (2015) *Strategic management in public organisations: Concepts, schools and contemporary issues*, London: Taylor & Francis.

George, B., Drumaux, A., Joyce, A. and Longo, F. (2020) 'Editoral', *Public Money and Management*, 40(4): 255–259.

Hamel, G. and Prahalad, C.K. (1994) *Competing for the future*, Boston: Harvard Business School Press.

Hansen, J.R. and Ferlie, E. (2014) 'Applying strategic management theories in public sector organizations: Developing a typology', *Public Management Review*, 18(1): 1–19.

Joyce, P. (2015) *Strategic management in the public sector*, London: Routledge.

Kasper, G., Marcoux, J., Folmer, K., Burleson, J., Evans, R., Holk, J., Brayton, S., Kanneganti, A., Haynesworth, L.J. and DeVera, D.J. (2020) 'An event or an era? Resources for social sector decision-making in the context of COVID-19', *Monitor Institute by Deloitte* [report], July 2020, available at: https://www2.deloitte.com/us/en/pages/about-deloitte/articles/covid-19-planning-scenarios-for-social-sector-organizations.html [Accessed 25 January 2022].

King's Fund (2020) *What are health inequalities?* [report], 18 February 2020, available at: https://www.kingsfund.org.uk/publications/what-are-health-inequalities [Accessed 25 January 2022].

Klijn, H.J. and Koppenjan, J. (2020) 'Strategic planning after the governance revolution', *Public Money and Management*, 40(4): 260–261.

McGuire, M. and Schneck, D. (2010) 'What if Hurricane Katrina hit in 2020? The need for strategic management of disasters', *Public Administration Review*, 70(1): S201–207.

Miles, R.E. and Snow, C.C. (1978) *Organizational strategy, structure and process*, New York: McGraw Hill.

Mintzberg, H., Ahlstrand, B. and Lampel, B. (1998) *Strategy safari: The complete guide through the wilds of strategic management*, London: Financial Times Prentice Hall.

Mulgan, G. (2009) *The art of public strategy: Mobilizing power and knowledge for the common good*, Oxford: Oxford University Press.

Mulgan, G. (2014) 'Innovation in the public sector', *NESTA* [report], November 2014, available at: https://www.nesta.org.uk/report/innovation-in-the-pub lic-sector/ [Accessed 25 January 2022].

Network Homes (2018) *5 year strategy 2018–2023* [report], updated May 2021, available at: https://www.networkhomes.org.uk/media/12182/5-year-strat egy-may-2021-final.pdf [Accessed 25 January 2022].

Organisation for Economic Co-operation and Development (2017) *Fostering innovation in the public sector*, Paris: OECD Publishing.

Porter, M.E. (1980) *Competitive strategy: Techniques for analyzing industries and competitors*, New York: Free Press.

Quirk, B. (2015) *High performing councils: Recipe not alchemy*, Cardiff: Public Policy Institute for Wales.

Whittington, R., Regnér, P., Johnson, G., Angwin, D. and Scholes, K. (2020) *Exploring strategy*, Harlow: Pearson.

World Bank (2008) *Brazil: Toward a more inclusive and effective participatory budget in Porto Alegre, volume 1. Main report*, Washington, DC: World Bank.

6

Leadership and management

David Phillips and Simon Read

Chapter objectives

Good public services must have effective management and strong leadership to meet current needs and anticipate future demand. Demand for public services is increasing and changing while budgets are rising slowly, if at all. To meet these challenges, public services are working in new ways. They engage with the public differently, adopt new technologies and develop collaborations. These collaborations often cross boundaries within and between organisations and increasingly involve the private sector. These changes frequently effect substantial procedural or cultural changes which demand good leadership and management. The relationship between leadership and management is often confused, and their definitions overlap. This chapter explores leadership and management in terms of their characteristics and benefits to teams and organisations. This includes considering where leadership sits, who can be a leader and how public services can develop good leadership and management. Throughout the chapter, leadership and management are placed in 'real world' contexts through a series of case studies for modern public service organisations.

Introduction

At first glance, leadership and management seem synonymous as both are about the exercise of authority. Weber (1947) describes three sources of authority. **Traditional authority** exists where a person's (or agency's) legitimacy comes from a society's customs or norms, such as social status (class) or association with a religion or belief system (the clergy, for example). This influence is not based on their knowledge or skill. While traditional authority continues today, as societal norms change, there are challenges to its legitimacy (Holm and Botlhale, 2008; Afaha, 2020). Afaha (2020) argues that the near-constant change of modern societies (commerce, communication and shifting populations) undermines traditional authority derived from the status quo. **Charismatic authority** exists where control stems from individual personality or perceived personality traits. Here, leaders gain influence because they are admired or respected for their perceived wisdom or understanding. Such people are often great orators and appeal to people's emotions (for example, their sense of justice, fairness, disadvantage or disillusionment). If charismatic authority is sustained from one person to another, it becomes institutionalised and incorporated into the traditional or rational regime (Rudolph and Rudolph, 1979). **Rational–legal authority** originates from an agreed set of rules, legal framework or constitution (for example, elected political leaders). In this case, leaders exercise the authority of their office and cease to have this authority when they lose office, for example with retirement or loss of an election. Various leadership and management models are underpinned by different forms of authority and assumptions about control, relationships and motivation.

The relationship between leadership and management is further muddled when looking at authority in the workplace and the interchangeable use of the terms. Some organisations have a *senior management team* while others have a *senior leadership team* performing the same role. Additionally, there may be a range of management titles, including supervisors and team leaders within an organisation. Kotter (1990: 3) was one of the first academics to distinguish between leadership (the ability to *mobilise* people) and leaders (people in positions of authority that are expected to provide leadership). It was this second use of leadership that he blamed for the confusion between it and management, which will be unpicked in this chapter. This chapter shows that leadership (*influence* and *relationships*) and management (*procedure*) are very different but equally important skill sets. Management is required so that public service organisations have a consistent environment (*processes* and *procedures*) for the public to engage with and so that workers know what is expected of them. Leadership stimulates and supports workers to thrive and motivates them to deliver the best public services possible. While success in one role gives no guarantee of success in the other, together, leadership and management can provide better conditions for workers and outcomes for the public. Ideas of leadership and management are essential to work in the public services. To understand this, the chapter first explores the origins of leadership and management theory and their modern adaptations. Then the relationship between leadership and management is examined, particularly in public services. Finally, new trends and developments in leadership and management that might aid public services are explored.

Understanding leadership

If leadership is about mobilising people, it is vital to understand how leaders do this. In public services, in particular, decisions need the foresight and flexibility to deal with planned or sudden changes (see Chapters 4 and 5). Different circumstances may require different styles.

Leadership theory

There are many leadership models, all of which explore how the relationship between leaders and followers works. Many of these are based on the work of Lewin and his colleagues (Lewin et al, 1939), which included three leadership styles: **autocratic**, **laissez-faire** and **democratic**.

Autocratic or **authoritarian** leaders make decisions and relay them to their team, relying on their own knowledge and expertise. It is often argued that autocratic decision making is fast and decisive because it eliminates time-consuming discussion or the need for consensus (Amanchukwu et al, 2015; Dyczkowska and Dyczkowski, 2018). This leadership style, however, ignores the knowledge and skills of other team members. It does nothing to imply they are valued and may result in a plan to which team members are indifferent.

In contrast, **laissez-faire** (*hands-off*) leadership, also known as **delegative** leadership, occurs when a leader devolves decision making to the team. This was initially described as a style with no leadership because workers are given little direction or support and are not held accountable (Lewin et al, 1939). Without supervision, the productivity of unmotivated, poorly skilled or insecure workers will decline alongside their morale, their sense of purpose and ability to work as a coherent team (Lewin et al, 1939). However, the development of highly effective teams can follow a path of increasing trust that allows for light-touch leadership. Leaders can be available, supportive and ultimately responsible for the team's welfare and success while giving them the space to apply their skills and knowledge.

A **democratic** or **participative** leader sets out the problem or goal to be addressed and then draws on the knowledge and skills of all team members to handle it. Thus, the democratic leader uses a more comprehensive knowledge base and makes better-informed decisions. The team will feel that their knowledge and skills are respected and helped to inform the plan adopted by the leader. As a result, the leadership and the team are pulling in the same direction with the same commitment. This is a slower process, requiring trust and open dialogue (Amanchukwu et al, 2015). It, therefore, lends itself to team building, and long-term and strategic developments (see Chapter 5). Lewin et al (1939) saw democratic leadership as the most productive style of leadership. It combines the advantages of the other leadership styles, notably effective organisation of the team and general buy-in to the team's objectives.

Change is one of the most significant risks to the performance of existing teams (see Chapter 4). Established relationships, tasks and work patterns may be disrupted without guaranteeing that workers will like the new arrangements. As a result, workers may be anxious about, or resistant or hostile to change. Democratic leadership addresses uncertainty through the workers' participation in analysing the problem and considering the options. As a result, workers understand the change and know managers have considered their views. Research suggests that workers involved in a transparent process that values their contributions are more likely to support change (O'Brien, 2002). Public services need strong leadership, but they also need effective management, which will be explored next, to meet current needs and prepare for future demands.

Understanding management

In contrast to leadership, which is about relationships with people, management is the procedural control of a team or organisation. Drucker (1974) sees management as undertaking a task with others. Koontz and Weihrich (2010: 5) describe management as 'designing and maintaining an environment in which individuals, working in groups, efficiently accomplish selected aims'. Managers have the authority to exercise control because of the office they hold. Their job title and organisational position give them the right to make decisions, give instructions and expect others to comply. Therefore, management is associated with rational-legal authority, the organisation of work or workers, and holding people accountable (Stewart, 1997); for example, Fayol (1949) describes the task of a manager as **controlling**, **planning**, **organising**, **commanding** and **coordinating**. The following subsection looks at classical management theories to contextualise modern management theory and explores the differences between management and leadership.

Classic theories about management

Classical management theory focuses on the efficient use of workers to maximise individual and organisational productivity. Pollitt (1997) and Nicotera (2019) argue that professional management arose in response to the shift from work in agriculture, and in artisan and small enterprises to a wage-based economy and large-scale organisations. These large-scale organisations sit outside, and undermine, the communal norms that regulated work before industrialisation. Thus, the organisation of workers on a large scale required people with management skills. Classical management theory assumes the relationship between workers and management is rational. Managers are motivated by profits (or cost reductions in the public sector) and workers by wages. Managers want to maximise worker output; workers wish to minimise their work effort (McGregor, 1960).

Social benefit, working conditions and job satisfaction are absent in classical management theories, or play a minor role (Fayol, 1949). Classical management theory is not concerned with developing a shared goal for managers and workers. Instead, a chain of command begins with direction setting at the top, middle managers translating strategy into actionable plans, and junior managers and workers implementing them. Communication runs in one direction from top to bottom, as instructions are broken down, circulated and followed. There is no requirement for skills or knowledge to be fed the other way, for workers to know the big picture or what other workers are doing. Finally, complex tasks are broken down into smaller functions repeatedly carried out by workers grouped according to their jobs. This idea of management matches authoritarian leadership. The development of classical management follows three increasingly sophisticated models developed in the first half of the 20th century: **scientific** (Taylor, 1997 [1911]), **administrative** (Fayol, 1949) and **bureaucratic** (Weber, 1947).

Taylor (1997 [1911]) advocates **scientific management**, sometimes known as **Taylorism**, in which managers deconstruct tasks to understand and carry out each element in the quickest and easiest way. Managers trial different techniques and evaluate them to select the fastest and easiest. The workers then carry out the job according to the method dictated by managers, with no input and no scope for deviation. Typically, this results in numerous workers being given individual sub-tasks that they repeat continuously. In contrast to an artisan, who would see a single task through from start to finish, these workers only need to be good at one sub-task.

Fayol's **administrative management theory**, also known as **Process Theory** or **Structural Theory**, published in 1916 in French, but first translated into English in 1949, goes beyond the performance of individual tasks to consider the management of organisations: organisational efficiency is a prerequisite to operational efficiency – poorly run organisations result in poor performance at every level (Fayol, 1949). An effective working relationship between managers and workers is critical for an effective organisation. Managers are assigned five broad roles, influenced by the culture (see Chapter 4) and the sector (see Chapter 2) in which organisations operate. **Planning** includes predicting future trends and demands, setting organisational objectives, developing strategies and plans to achieve these objectives, and responding to future needs (see Chapter 5). **Organising** involves the development of appropriate structures and procedures, bringing workers, training and equipment together. **Command**, or supervision and motivation of workers, is critical. In addition to commanding workers, managers need to **coordinate** workers' efforts, for example, across teams. Finally, they need to **control** workers to ensure what is delivered follows set plans.

Fayol (1949) established 14 principles to aid managers in these roles, some of which are particularly important for public services. The organisational structure gives managers the **authority** to make decisions and expect compliance, holding workers to account. As with Taylorism, the **division of labour** and the specialism of workers in sub-tasks, the **discipline** of workers and respect for managers, and the **subordination of individual interest** are all essential. Managers and workers need to put personal agendas to the side. Unity of **command** and **direction** ensure clear communication of goals, strategies and instructions. Consistent lines of communication, with instructions always coming via the same route and reports returning in the opposite direction, maintain hierarchy and, authority and prevent duplication or contradiction. This means every team is pulling in the same direction, and every worker understands management desires. Good communication, clear **lines of authority** (**scalar chains**) and accountability are essential parts of an effective organisation.

Fayol's (1949) model also sees the relationship between managers and workers as rational and dependent upon **remuneration**. Managers can reward and incentivise workers, normally financially, but other means can also be used. Order is achieved, at least partly, by **equity** (applying fair rules) and **stability of tenure**, as only long-standing workers can appreciate the benefits of working in this environment. Stability of tenure ensures workers are interested in the employer's long-term success or develop a sense of loyalty and commitment. A resulting sense of attachment or belonging, *esprit de corps* or team spirit, will encourage workers to do their best for the organisation. In this context, worker initiative is encouraged to find solutions to problems that managers can adopt. Fayol's (1949) model remains authoritarian, but there is a nascent understanding that workers are not exclusively motivated by wages and can identify with the organisation's success.

Weber (1947) developed **Bureaucratic Management Theory** as a model of rational, rule-based administration based on security, hierarchy and the selection of workers and managers based on competence. Bureaucratic Management is an evolution from traditional (based on values, emotion and past precedent) to modern (technically based) management. Not only is it more efficient, the rational-legal basis also provides a more sustainable source of legitimacy than traditional or charismatic authority. The appeal of charismatic leaders is greatest during a crisis and therefore unsustainable, as it wanes when the crisis passes and the emotional appeal declines (Weber, 1947). Therefore, Weber (1997) emphasises the importance of the separation of politicians (or business owners) from impartial administrators (public service managers and workers). Similarly, administrators achieve impartiality by separating the personal (private life, views and personal interests) from the official (acting for the organisation's benefit). This was ingrained in the public services in the UK by the Committee on Standards in Public Life (1995) in *The Seven Principles of Public Life*. Weber's rational-legal model (1997) seeks to achieve consistency and impartiality and ensure decision makers are qualified for their role with mechanisms to guarantee this and address failings. Workers accept the manager's authority to make decisions and give instructions because of the rational basis. Based on the model, managers are competent and operate exclusively within their assigned roles. Workers and more junior managers accept decisions and comply with the instructions of their seniors (but with recourse to more senior management when managers misbehave). Obedience is owed to the office, not the individual, and is restricted to roles within the hierarchy.

Modern management

Modern management theory, from the 1960s onwards, builds on classic management theory, addressing perceived weaknesses in some classical assumptions and exploring effectiveness of different management styles. It questions whether workers only act in their personal interest or are influenced by group dynamics in the workplace and beyond. Can tasks be disaggregated and organised in isolation within organisations? While leadership motivates workers, it is management that gives them the tools, processes and procedures, including lines of communication and accountability, to perform tasks to comply with the organisational plans and strategies (see Chapter 5).

Elton Mayo (2003 [1933]) was part of the **behavioural school** of management and a founder of Human Relations Management. Despite being a contemporary of the classical theorists, he is generally grouped with modern management theorists. Elton Mayo challenges the classical assumption that employment relationships are based on management's need to push worker productivity and workers' wishes to minimise effort. He argues that alongside the formal structure of the workplace, an informal social structure exists, which influences workers' behaviour. Workers are not motivated exclusively by a utilitarian aim to maximise income while minimising effort. Classical management theory underplays the value of social engagement and non-financial rewards, leading managers to neglect the impact of good morale on productivity. Based on a series of experiments from the 1920s, Elton Mayo indicated that changing the organisation of work (shift patterns and breaks) and providing positive feedback and encouragement led to a reduction in staff turnover and improved productivity.

Like Elton Mayo, **systems thinking**, when applied to management, looks at relationships within an organisation but sees organisations as elements of a broader system (Chikere and Nwoka, 2015). The complex structure and the importance of interaction between the components (network) are emphasised by von Bertalanffy (1968). For example, a public service organisation might be part of a sector (education or housing) or a larger organisation (local, devolved or central government), but the organisation is a part of both systems. The openness of von Bertalanffy's model includes elements outside the organisation, which is opposed to the closed system of classical management models that only consider internal organisational workings. Systems thinking is key, as external forces impact internal dynamics (see Chapters 1 and 4). If managers ignore these, they miss threats and opportunities (see Chapter 5). However, systems thinking also addresses criticism that the disaggregation of tasks ignores the relationships between the internal parts of the organisation. Internally, coordination, synergy and collaboration are needed to prevent change in one area from causing problems in another. For example, a public housing organisation might have competing goals (see Chapter 1) with strategies promoting higher building standards and the re-use of brownfield sites, which contribute to higher building costs on the one hand and a strategy to promote the expansion of affordable housing on the other. A systems approach would consider strategies collectively so that they support rather than conflict with each other.

The systems approach also addresses concerns that classical management models ignore the social nature of workplaces. The holistic nature of the systems approach requires consideration of the technical and social variables in and of the system, as a change in either may result in a shift in the other. From a systemic view, management is a social activity that is cognitive, empathic and conducted through relationships (Tate, 2009). In this model, managers need to have a clear personal understanding of both internal and external systems. This requires clear and regular feedback processes that respond to service users and workers. All actors within an organisation need to be considered in a process that allows flexibility, continuous improvement, organisational learning and the ability to handle uncertainty. Given the environment in which public services operate (see Chapters 1, 4 and 5), this approach allows managers a clear means of strategic planning.

Bringing management and leadership together

Combining management and leadership approaches can meet the needs of managers and workers and create a shared view of success. Management theories are often a response to procedurally driven approaches that focus on the organisation of work and workers. In contrast, leadership theories emphasise creativity, the social aspects of work and workers, and their potential to contribute solutions.

McGregor (1960) characterised these two approaches as **Theory X** and **Theory Y**. Theory X is based on the utilitarian understanding of the classical management theories, where wages are the main reward for work and workers are motivated solely by remuneration. The relationship between workers and managers or leaders is transactional. Consequently, managers need to supervise workers constantly, as they will take on no more work or responsibility than they have to. The management and leadership approach that Theory X advocates is often referred to as *carrot and stick*, for example using performance-related pay and bonuses. In contrast, Theory Y sees workers as self-motivated and believes that they thrive on responsibility. Their rewards for participating in work are financial, social and self-actualising. Work brings purpose, status, self-respect and pride. Advocates of Theory Y trust their workers, delegate authority and responsibility, and encourage self-improvement. Moreover, managers and leaders adhering to Theory Y encourage workers to be part of the problem–solving and decision-making process. Theory Y encourages democratic leaders and systems thinkers to consider the human aspects of the environment and the social aspects of work, for example, with regular team meetings discussing challenges and potential solutions. They do this for pragmatic rather than altruistic reasons, believing that this improves performance. Theories X and Y are the exact antitheses of each other. Affiliation to one or the other of these theories determines managerial and leadership styles and a unique balance between management (*procedure*) and leadership (*influence*). In the following, discussions about **transactional**, **transformational** and **situational** leadership are placed in this context.

Transactional leadership (Weber, 1947) is an X theory based on exchange (or *transaction*), which is a procedural approach to leadership rooted in classical management theory. It assumes that workers and managers know their roles and conform to them. In return, managers can rely on workers' labour and workers receive a wage. There may also be penalties for challenging management and benefits associated with compliance; for example, those who have complied may receive praise, bonus payments or promotion. There is no mechanism for workers to contribute to or challenge decisions made by management. People follow managers because of the benefits of doing so and the costs associated with not doing so. In addition, there is little scope and no incentive for the followers to try new ideas or take risks because failure will be punished (for example, loss of bonuses), and the status quo is already rewarded. X theory leadership requires careful monitoring of workers for appropriate rewards and punishments, as seen in public services with New Public Management (see Chapter 4). Transactional leadership also involves the maintenance of a power difference. It sits well with lines of authority and accountability (Fayol) or hierarchical control (Weber) where power relationships are built into the system. If transactional leadership is leadership at all, then it is authoritarian because these leaders are dependent on management mechanisms to support their authority. This is common within large public services where decision making is remote from delivery, but less so in smaller organisations, for example in voluntary sector organisations delivering public services.

In contrast, Theory Y approaches draw more on Lewin's democratic leadership style and ideas of **transformational leadership**. Transformational leadership is based around the idea of team-based working to identify needed changes while constructing a vision to guide that change (Burns, 1978; Bass, 1985). Transformational leadership is intended to be inspirational, inclusive and motivational, drawing on non-financial rewards to motivate workers; for example, worker commitment to addressing social problems (youth work, education) or serving the greater good (for example, when serving in the military). Some scholars indicate that it improves performance and job satisfaction, and leads to increased loyalty (Bass, 1985). Transformational leadership requires leaders to have a clear vision, persuade others to take on that vision as their own, and engage others in creating shared meaning (Bennis, 2009). It requires leaders to empathise with their workers, be attuned to them, and feel their pain, wants and needs. Leaders also need a distinctive voice, purpose, self-confidence and a sense of self. They need to have integrity, character and a clear moral compass aided by the belief in something outside oneself. Such leaders pay significant attention to *human resources* at their command, recognising them as one of the most important assets available to deliver the organisation's goal. Their role often involves more influence (leadership), but they tend to neglect procedure (management) at their peril.

Situational or **contingency theory** starts from the premise that, in practice, each style of management or leadership has benefits and may be suitable in some circumstances. It involves leaders applying different management and leadership styles according to the circumstances and the needs of the people they are working with. Leading situationally means offering teams the right amount of support or direction at the right time rather than using one leadership style regardless of circumstances. This requires situational awareness, the perception of the internal and external environments (see Chapter 5) and events around them, understanding their meaning, and the projection of their future status (see Box 6.1), which overlaps with a systems approach. This is important in the public services when tackling a **wicked issue** (see Chapter 1) that requires innovation, such as promoting equality, mitigating environmental challenges and climate change (see Chapters 8, 9 and 10).

Box 6.1: Situational awareness in the armed forces

The armed forces are a key part of public services in the UK. They have a distinct form of decision making for leaders drawing on the idea of **Operational Estimates**, which comes in seven stages. This draws on critical ideas of **situational awareness**.

- Stage 1: Review the situation, creating a high level of situational awareness, ensuring that the team has a common understanding of the background and underlying causes of the problem. Similar approaches are also applied in emergency services.
- Stage 2: Identify and analyse the problem to clearly understand, solve or lessen its impact.
- Stage 3: Leaders must then create a plan to focus staff effort and to inform analysis of potential solutions.
- Stage 4: Then develop and validate a course of action, including measurable milestones and set points to review progress. This is similar to risk analysis techniques, which also aid situational awareness.
- Stage 5: An evaluation of the proposed plan then gives the leader the best possible option. This will also form the basis for a 'lessons learnt' document to aid future development.
- Stage 6: The leader selects options and develops the plan in depth, turning the concept into a workable plan while linking it to organisational values, visions and goals.
- Stage 7: Post-operational assessment identifies experiences, examples and observations that contribute to future tasks and operations. Success is based on rapid and relevant learning to improve the next cycle of operations.

Trends and developments

The long-term trend in management theory is to include more leadership in the control of teams and organisations, shifting from Theory X to Theory Y, and public services are at the forefront of this movement. Applying the principles of Theory Y (considering the human and social aspects of work) to leadership and management in public services helps create responsive organisations that react well to complex issues. However, it does rely on empathy to create safe environments for team members to participate freely, particularly at the ideas stage.

Design thinking is an iterative process whereby the desired results are achieved through repeated calculated trial and error cycles (Brown and Wyatt, 2010). Leaders (or managers) can use this approach to manage (or lead) change and promote innovation, both of which are critical challenges in public services. Design thinking allows managers to draw on their staff's, and even service users', perceptions, knowledge and expertise to maximise new ideas (see Box 6.2). They can also be included in change management (see Chapter 4), making change less threatening and more acceptable (even if not genuinely welcome). Design thinking enables leadership in new ways and should not be considered in isolation; for example, it could be linked to transformational leadership and systems thinking. These principles focus on the leader facilitating crucial conversations, accessing powerful questions and removing barriers in the public service environment. This enables workers to support problem solving and sometimes to find their own answers in a safe and supported environment. The development of such an environment is often referred to as **compassionate leadership**.

Box 6.2: Design thinking in practice: housing services in Wales

Design thinking approaches, drawn from the design industry, accept that workers are, or can be, creative and require managers to empathise with their team. This approach asks managers to be aware of their own perceptions, assumptions and prejudices and be open to other perceptions of the problem. Managers observe and learn from how the team engages with the task and environment. Managers may define the questions for consideration, setting out the big picture and vision, for example improved outcomes in day surgery. However, the team will help generate the specifics at the ideation stage, so options are developed that benefit from the team's broader expertise and achieve general buy-in from the group. Finally, the innovation or change is tested, evaluated and, if appropriate, rolled out. Design thinking allowed existing service users and the staff at Neath Port Talbot Housing (now Tai Tarion) to review support for older tenants so that it was better targeted. The inclusive nature of the process ensured that the people who were most anxious about the changes had substantial control, understood the changes and supported them (Gallagher and Dineen, 2015).

Although **compassionate leadership** has existed since the 1990s, it has grown in prominence in recent years. Championed by health services worldwide and particularly in the UK, compassionate leadership is firmly rooted in a Theory Y vision. It requires managers to step up to leadership and provide workers with the environment and support to thrive. West (2021) argues that compassionate leadership is challenging and needs brave leaders prepared to hear things they do not want to hear, whether from staff or service users. The four core behaviours of compassionate leadership are: **attending** to others; **understanding** and **empathising** with other people's situations; and taking intelligent action to **help**. Compassionate leadership is a culture that needs to be embedded across a team or organisation. Everyone is then responsible for the development of this culture and leadership becomes collective, shifting from managers to the whole team. However, leaders have a special role in signalling the team's culture to others. Goleman et al (2001) argue that a leader's emotions are contagious and need to contain energy and enthusiasm for public service organisations to thrive. It is therefore important to ensure future public service leaders are compassionate, innovative and collaborative in their approach to address future challenges.

Summary

Management and leadership are different concepts, addressing different needs in modern public service organisations. Indeed, a combination of the two provides the best opportunity for staff to thrive and for public services to be the best they can be. Management provides the structure of organisations, the processes and procedures that create continuity and stability for workers and service users alike. In classical management models, there is an assumed relationship between managers and workers based on the manager's authority to give instructions and expect compliance in return for a wage. Modern management theory challenges the simple transactional motivation, pointing to other benefits of work – financial, social and self-actualising. Modern management theory offers the possibility that workers can be motivated and rewarded in different ways and included in problem-solving exercises.

In contrast, leadership, the ability to mobilise followers, is based on respect and thus influence over worker behaviour. Nonetheless, leadership may be authoritarian, with instructions given and obeyed, or democratic, where leaders draw upon the knowledge and skills of workers to support decision making and problem solving. These alternatives give rise to McGregor's (1960) alternative X (transactional/authoritarian) and Y (democratic) theories. These theories allow transactional theories (classic management and authoritarian leadership) and transformational theories (systems thinking and democratic leadership) to be brought together. In doing so, the contradiction between leadership and management ends, and the synergy between styles is highlighted in its place.

Key points

- Leadership and management are about the exercise of authority.
- The way that authority is used depends on the leadership or management style chosen.
- Leadership and management are separate concepts, but public service organisations need to consider approaches to both to be effective.

Questions

- To what extent is leadership a function of authority?
- How do classical management models compare to modern models?
- Under what circumstances might transactional leadership work best in public services?
- Under what circumstances might transformational leadership work best in public services?

Further reading

Grint, K. (2010) *Leadership: A very short introduction*, Oxford: Oxford University Press. *This book explores the why, what and who of leadership and outlines different leadership styles.*

Thompson, J.L., Scott, J.M. and Martin, F. (2014) *Strategic management: Awareness and change* (7th edn), Boston: Cengage Learning. *This book explores the connection between management and strategic decision making.*

References

Afaha, P. (2020) 'Authority conflicts and the declining influence of traditional rulers in north-western Nigeria', *International Journal of Humanitatis Theoreticus*, 3(1): 239–250.

Amanchukwu, R.N., Stanley, G.J. and Ololube, N.P. (2015) 'A review of leadership theories, principles and styles and their relevance to educational management', *Management 2015*, 5(1): 6–14.

Bass, B.M. (1985) *Leadership and performance beyond expectations*, New York: Free Press.

Bennis, W.G. (2009) *On becoming a leader*, New York: Basic Books.

Brown, T. and Wyatt, J. (2010) 'Design thinking for social innovation', *Stanford Social Innovation Review*, Winter: 31–35.

Burns, J.M. (1978) *Leadership*, New York: Harper & Row.

Chikere, C.C. and Nwoka, J. (2015) 'The systems theory of management in modern organizations: A study of Aldgate Congress Resort Limited Port Harcourt', *International Journal of Scientific and Research Publications*, 5(9): 1–7.

Committee on Standards in Public Life (1995) *The seven principles of public life*, London: HMSO.

Drucker, P.F. (1974) *Management*, London: Heinemann Professional.

Dyczkowska, J. and Dyczkowski, T. (2018) 'Democratic or autocratic leadership style? Participative management and its links to rewarding strategies and job satisfaction in SMEs', *Athens Journal of Business & Economics*, 4(2): 193–218.

Elton Mayo, G. (2003 [1933]) *The human problems of an industrial civilization*, Abingdon: Routledge.

Fayol, H. (1949) *General and industrial management* (trans C. Storrs), London: Sir Isaac Pitman & Sons.

Gallagher, M. and Dineen, R. (2015) *Co-production catalogue for Wales: Seeing is believing*, Cardiff: Public Health Wales/Co-production Wales.

Goleman, D., Boyatzis, R. and McKee, A. (2001) 'Primal leadership: The hidden driver of great performance', *Harvard Business Review*, December: 42–51.

Holm, J.D. and Botlhale, E. (2008) 'Persistence and decline of traditional authority in modern Botswana politics', *Botswana Notes and Records*, 40: 74–87.

Koontz, H. and Weihrich, H. (2010) *Essentials of management: An international perspective* (8th edn), New Dehli: Tata McGraw-Hill.

Kotter, J.P. (1990) *A force for change: How leadership differs from management*, London: Collier Macmillan.

Lewin, K., Lippitt, R. and White, R.K. (1939) 'Patterns of aggressive behaviour in experimentally created "social climates"', *Journal of Social Psychology*, 10(2): 271–299.

McGregor, D. (1960) *The human side of enterprise*, London: McGraw-Hill.

Nicotera, A. (2019) 'Classical management theory', in Nicotera, A. (ed.), *Origins and traditions of organizational communication*, Abingdon: Routledge, pp 89–105.

O'Brien, G. (2002) 'Participation as the key to successful change: A public sector case study', *Leadership & Organization Development Journal*, 23(8): 442–455.

Pollitt, C. (1997) 'The development of management thought', in Hill, M. (ed.), *The policy process: A reader*, London: Routledge, pp 328–339.

Rudolph, L.I. and Rudolph, S. (1979) 'Authority and power in bureaucratic and patrimonial administration: Revisionist interpretation of Weber on bureaucracy', *World Politics*, 31(2): 195–227.

Stewart, R. (1997) *The reality of management* (3rd edn), Oxford: Butterworth-Heinemann.

Tate, W. (2009) *The search for leadership: An organisational perspective*, Charmouth: Triarchy Press.

Taylor, F.W. (1997 [1911]) *The principles of scientific management*, Mineola: Dover Publications.

Von Bertalanffy, L. (1968) *The meaning of general systems theory*, New York: George Braziller.

Weber, M. (1947) *Theory of social and economic organization* (trans A.M. Henderson and T. Parsons), New York: Free Press.

Weber, M. (1997) 'Rational–legal authority and bureaucracy', in Hill, M. (ed.), *The policy process: A reader*, London: Routledge, pp 323–327.

West, M.A. (2021) *Compassionate leadership: Sustaining wisdom, humanity and presence in health and social care*, London: The Swirling Leaf Press.

PART III

Achieving social and environmental impact

7

Public services and the challenge of sustainability

E.K. Sarter

Chapter objectives

The idea of sustainability is becoming increasingly widespread. This chapter explores sustainability and its importance for public services. It shows that while sustainability was initially confined to a narrow understanding that focused on environmental considerations only, today it is commonly understood as a multifaceted concept that encompasses economic, social and environmental considerations. The relationship between these three aspects is thereby not without challenges. Against the background of increasing concerns about the environmental crisis and global injustices, sustainability is gaining importance as a guideline for policies and a consideration for public services. Thereby, public procurement has received particular attention. Taking public procurement as an example, this chapter explores the move towards sustainability and the challenges that arise when putting sustainability into practice. This chapter concludes with an exploration of trends and developments in fostering sustainability.

Introduction

Over the past decades, sustainability has gained growing importance. International, regional, national and subnational initiatives aim to promote sustainability. One of the most important among these initiatives is the 2030 Agenda for Sustainable Development. Adopted by all member states of the United Nations (UN), it outlines 17 **Sustainable Development Goals** (**SDGs**), which seek, among others, to eradicate hunger and poverty, promote good health, wellbeing and quality education, reduce inequality, ensure clean water and sanitation, and clean and affordable energy, and to foster decent work and economic growth as well as responsible production and consumption. Since their adoption in 2015, the SDGs have been an influential driver for sustainability and have influenced the work of the UN and its agencies as well as organisations such as the Organisation for Economic Co-operation and Development (OECD) and states. Further initiatives at different levels aim to promote sustainability. The OECD, for instance, has issued several recommendations and guides, particularly relating to the environmental performance of the public sector. The Global Reporting Initiative seeks to promote sustainability reporting, among others, but not exclusively in the public sector. Reporting is essential for taking stock of the current situation and to track performance. It thereby is a core part of accountability (see Chapter 4). Promoting sustainable development is not restricted to international or regional initiatives and organisations. National governments have increasingly embraced sustainability as a core concern of policymaking and implementation. The drive towards a more sustainable future in general is reflected not only in strategic plans, such as the German *Nachhaltigkeitsstrategie*, the French *Stratégie nationale de développement durable*, or the UK's sustainability plan. It also led to a growth in public policies and initiatives aiming at strengthening sustainability in public policies at national and subnational level, such as the Well-being of Future Generations (Wales) Act 2015 (see Box 7.1) introduced in Wales in 2015.

Box 7.1: Well-being of Future Generations Act

The Well-being of Future Generations (WFG) Act, a Welsh piece of legislation, was adopted in 2015 and aims to promote sustainable development. Focused on engaging public bodies as drivers for change, the WFG obliges public bodies in Wales to adopt a long-term perspective, to consider the social, cultural, economic and environmental impacts of their action, and to promote sustainable development. Applying to a range of public bodies – from the Welsh Government and local authorities to local Health Boards, Fire and Rescue Authorities, and Sport Wales – the WFG imposes the duty to consider the principles of sustainable development on public services. It sets out seven Well-being Goals:

- a prosperous Wales;
- a resilient Wales;
- a healthier Wales;
- a more equal Wales;
- a Wales of cohesive communities;
- a Wales of vibrant culture and thriving Welsh language; and
- a globally responsible Wales.

In accordance with the principle of sustainability, the WFG requires public bodies to consider these goals 'as an integrated set of seven' (Welsh Government, 2016: 26). In addition, the WFG outlines five ways of working, a long-term perspective, prevention, integration, collaboration and involvement. By committing public bodies (including public services such as the fire service) to working towards sustainability, the WFG shapes the goals that public services work towards and

---

calls for increased attention to these areas. At the same time, it affects their way of working, and commits them to adopting a longer-term vision and preventive action, and to fostering collaboration between different services as well as with citizens and other organisations.

One particular concern in relation to promoting sustainability is public purchasing of goods, works and services (public procurement), which accounts for an important part of government spending and is an area in which a range of public services are actively engaged. Different international, regional, national and subnational organisations, associations and initiatives, as well as states and subnational entities, have taken an interest in socially responsible and sustainable public procurement. In addition to the general sustainability initiatives mentioned earlier, specific initiatives such as the UN's Guiding Principles on Business and Human Rights (UNGPs) aim to promote sustainability or specific aspects relating to it (for example respect for human rights or environmental aspects) in and through public procurement. The UNGPs, for example, specifically call on states to work towards ensuring that the enterprises they have commercial relationships with respect human rights. This includes the strategic use of public procurement (UN, 2011).

This chapter examines the idea of sustainability, its history, meaning and challenges with particular focus on public services. The first part explores the term and the idea of sustainability, its development and growing importance. Based on these general insights into sustainability, the second part explores the challenges of acting more sustainably in one particular field, public procurement. It explores the tensions between the drive to foster sustainable procurement practices on the one hand and demands on and constraints of (public) resources on the other. Having explored sustainability broadly and with a focus on public service procurement, the third part highlights trends and developments in both areas.

Sustainability: a multidimensional concept

Considerations of the environmental impact of human actions and sustainable agricultural practices have been evidenced for a long time. People all over the world have devised strategies to sustain the environment and limit harmful human impact. Farmers, for instance, have strategically used crop rotation to increase productivity and allow the land to recover. While considering the environmental impact of human actions has a long history, it was not until the early 18th century that the concept of sustainability was born. In 1713, Hans Carl von Carlowitz coined the German term *Nachhaltigkeit* to denote a model of forestry where only as many trees are cut as can grow back. Since then, the term and the concept of sustainability gained increasing prominence and spread across languages and countries. From its original application in the field of forestry, over the centuries (especially since the second half of the 20th century) the concept of sustainability expanded beyond the boundaries of agriculture.

Today, sustainability is widely understood as a multidimensional concept that encompasses environmental, economic and social aspects. The most commonly used definition of sustainability and sustainable development goes back to the 1980s, when in 1987 the World Commission on Environment and Development, the so-called Brundtland Commission, issued its report *Our Common Future*. In this report, the Brundtland Commission highlighted the importance of the environment, the economy and the social as three dimensions of sustainability (sometimes also labelled aspects, pillars, perspectives, and so on). More specifically, it defined sustainable development as 'development that meets the needs of the present without compromising the ability of future generations to meet their own needs' (World Commission on Environment and Development, 1987: 24). The Brundtland Commission's report highlights two core ideas that remain central to the concept of sustainability. Firstly, the crucial importance of satisfying essential needs (particularly those of 'the world's poor' [World Commission on Environment and Development, 1987: 54], whose basic needs for shelter, food or income remained unaddressed) and secondly, doing so within the boundaries of the earth's ecological limitations. At the same time, *Our Common Future* already set out the multidimensional nature of sustainability and the interrelatedness of social, economic and environmental developments. Ten years after the Brundtland Commission's report, the UN's Resolution *Agenda for Development* (51/240) highlighted the multidimensional nature of sustainability when stating that '[e]conomic development, social development and environmental protection are interdependent and mutually reinforcing components of sustainable development' (UN, 1997: 12). While different interpretations of sustainability exist, this definition of sustainability, which integrates economic, social and environmental considerations as interacting and interdependent aspects, has gained considerable acceptance and is the most widely used one today.

The need to reconcile the economy, the social and the environment lies at the heart of the idea and the concept of sustainability. This need arises from the perception of human individuals, economic practices and the environment as separate entities, a perception that is deeply rooted in Western thought and tradition. In contrast to modern Western thought, which sees humans and the surrounding environment as separate entities, other, especially Indigenous, cultures display a different understanding of the relationship between human individuals, communities and the environment. In general, Indigenous cultures and thought tend to see humans and their environment as deeply interrelated and interdependent. It is hence from the modern Western perception that conceptualises humans, their social and economic actions, and the environment as separate entities that the necessity for reconciliation arises. Against this background, the concept of sustainability and the problems it addresses can be seen as 'a product of Western thinking' (Mazzocchi, 2020: 78).

Sustainability challenges: from the tragedy of the commons to conflicts and trade-offs

While sustainability has gained traction and is becoming an increasingly important issue for public services, acting sustainably does not come without challenges. Before exploring a specific area of public activity in more detail, it is vital to examine key challenges at a more general level.

Hardin (1968) published 'The tragedy of the commons', an article that proved influential for debates on sustainability and environmental issues. In it, he argued that individual benefits and sustainability of shared land and resources, which belong to the community (the commons), were at odds as each individual using the commons is embedded in a system that encourages seeking one's own benefit, even at the cost of the sustainability of the commons. Drawing on the example of common pastures, Hardin (1968: 1244) argued that 'the rational herdsman concludes that the only sensible course for him to pursue is to add another animal to his herd. And another; and another. ... But this is the conclusion reached by each and every rational herdsman sharing a commons'. As a result of each actor's focus on their own benefit rather than the viability of the common resource, the common becomes overgrazed and unviable. Consequently, Hardin concludes that 'freedom of the commons means at the same time their "ruin"' (Hardin, 1968: 1244).

While the idea of the tragedy of commons that Hardin outlined has shaped debates on sustainability and the environment in particular, subsequent empirical research raises important criticisms and doubts about this assumption. Ostrom most importantly questioned the underlying assumptions of isolated individuals focusing only on their own benefit. Moreover, in her empirical work (1990; 2000), for which she won the Nobel Prize for Economics, Ostrom draws on a range of empirical examples showing that effective local and community governance of pooled resources is not only possible but does exist in practice.

As mentioned earlier, the concept of sustainability highlights the interconnectedness of the different dimensions it encompasses. The interaction between the different dimensions is not always without conflict. Rather, environmental considerations, social concerns and economic aims can (and oftentimes do) display a conflictual relationship. Take the example of economic growth; economic growth is often assumed to be a crucial pathway towards the alleviation of poverty. Economic growth, however, generates environmental costs, from the use of environmental resources to the production of waste and emissions (see Chapter 9). While promoting economic growth can generate positive economic and social impacts, it may at the same time result in negative environmental outcomes. These may in turn affect humans negatively, reducing the initially stated positive social impact. Whether or not trade-offs between the three dimensions can be accepted is a disputed topic. Two main approaches exist, commonly denoted as weak and strong sustainability. **Strong sustainability** rests on the assumption that trade-offs should be avoided or at least remain highly limited. In contrast, **weak sustainability** assumes that trade-offs between the dimensions can be made.

Sustainability in practice: a focus on public purchasing

In the wake of growing attention paid to sustainability, the purchase of goods, works and services by public bodies, **public procurement**, has received significant attention. Public procurement is of major economic importance; in 2017, it accounted for 29.1 per cent of total government expenditure and about 12 per cent of GDP in the OECD (OECD, 2019: 134). Given high amounts of money spent, public bodies are important consumers, who can strategically use public contracts to support the development of social enterprises, thereby supporting their goals. They can also strategically use their spending power to create or support markets for sustainable goods and services. This opens new opportunities for income for companies producing or delivering these sustainable goods or services. Therefore, it has been argued that strategic public consumption can be an important stepping stone in creating a business case for sustainability by offering companies an economic incentive to fulfil the sustainability requirements that allow them to access profitable public contracts (Steurer et al, 2012). Increasingly, public contracts incorporate environmental standards and social requirements relating, for example, to working conditions, wages and equality. With a growing importance of public purchasing and an increasing tendency to incorporate standards, public contracts are important tools for regulation. They lay down basic requirements and targets for the services purchased. As public contracts (can) incorporate requirements relating to wages and/or qualifications, they also become an important factor that influences wages and qualification levels of staff delivering publicly contracted services (Sarter and Karamanidou, 2019).

Before turning to explore sustainability and public procurement, it is vital to understand that public services can take different roles in public procurement processes. First, public services can be the actor initiating and carrying out a public procurement process. This would, for instance, be the case when a public service organisation, such as the police, buys an item, for example uniforms. When public services are the buyer of a good, works project or a service, they shape and define the public procurement process. In contrast to a situation where a public service is the buyer, public services can also be the object that is being purchased. Take the example of public services which are provided by voluntary or private sector entities on behalf of the government (see Introduction and Chapter 2). Here, a public contract, which is the result of a public procurement process, is the foundation upon which a specific service is purchased from and delivered by an external organisation. For public services, which are publicly purchased, public procurement practices have important implications; they shape the services themselves, for example by influencing the available resources and setting regulatory standards and targets.

Principal-agent theory focuses on situations where, like in public procurement, one actor (the principal) delegates a task to another actor, or actors, who acts on their behalf (the agent), who may then delegate it further to subagent(s). The principal's decisions can influence the incentives for the agent, just as the agent's decisions influence the incentives for the subagent. Principal and agent (and if existent, subagents) have different preferences and interests. Information is distributed asymmetrically between the parties (Gailmard, 2014). Should the interests diverge sufficiently, a conflict of interest arises. If the agent holds considerably more information than the principal this increases the risk that the agent acts in their own – rather than the principal's – interest or even at the principal's expense. The same holds true for subagents. To address this, principals typically revert to supervisory strategies, most importantly to monitoring and bonding measures, which are 'intended to ensure that the agent sticks to the objectives' (Hannes, 2007: 1439).

Sustainable public procurement

Laws and policies (see Chapters 1 and 3 for a general outline of the importance of laws and policies) are important factors shaping public procurement choices; they can require, enable or hinder sustainable public procurement practices. Public procurement is an area that is regulated by a multilevel legal framework, encompassing international, regional, national and, in some cases, subnational regulation. The first international regulation of public procurement, passed in 1949, was the International Labour Organization's Labour Clauses (Public Contracts) Convention. It outlines minimum standards regarding working conditions in public contracts for signatory states. In contrast, the Agreement on Government Procurement (GPA), a plurilateral agreement situated within the framework of the World Trade Organization, focuses on market building, and aims to open public procurement markets between signatory states. It sets out rules that aim to ensure open, fair and transparent competition in public procurement for specified procurement activities. Of particular importance in this context are transparency and non-discrimination of tenderers.

Today, the European Union provides the most comprehensive regional framework of public procurement. It is grounded in the four freedoms (free movement of goods; free movement of capital; freedom to establish and provide services; and free movement of persons), which have formed part of the legal framework since the beginning of the European project. More specific secondary law on public procurement emerged since the 1970s. As is the case for the GPA, transparency and non-discrimination among tenderers are also cornerstones of European public procurement regulation. Within this context, social and environmental aspects can form part of public purchasing; this is placed under the condition that they must not contradict the principles of transparency and non-discrimination and that they are linked to the subject matter of the contract. Early on, when explicit regulation on this was absent, the European Court of

Justice had established this repeatedly. Over time, European regulations explicitly acknowledged the possibility to take environmental and social aspects into account (Sarter, 2015).

Public procurement regulation further exists at national and, in some countries such as Germany or the UK, at subnational level. With concerns about the environmental, social and economic impact of production and consumption practices and the impact of oftentimes opaque global value chains with frequently exploitative working conditions, there has been a rise in national and/or subnational legislation to promote sustainable public procurement in countries like Germany, Sweden and the Netherlands. Thereby, public procurement regulation does not always refer to sustainable public procurement as such but may relate to different aspects, which can be conceived as part of sustainability (for example, requirements relating to emissions, energy efficiency, human rights, and decent working conditions in global production chains and so on).

Sustainable public purchasing between cost considerations and social impact

Recent years have seen an increasing drive towards sustainable practices in general and sustainable public procurement more specifically. However, implementing sustainable public procurement practices does not come without challenges. One of the major challenges lies in the tension between the different dimensions of sustainability. To fully capture this, it is essential to visualise the context within which public procurement choices are made.

Since the 1980s, growing budgetary constraints and a paradigm of the superiority of business practices contributed to a trend towards marketisation, shared among Western welfare states over the last few decades. In the wake of mounting concerns about budgetary constraints and the growing importance of the paradigm of New Public Management, contracting out of services and public procurement have gained increasing importance (Pollitt and Bouckaert, 2011; see also Chapters 2 and 4). These developments (growing budgetary constraints and marketisation of services) have been important for three reasons. First, increased marketisation contributed to a growing importance of public procurement, particularly of services. Second, budgetary constraints and increased concerns with public spending set a tight framework for public bodies' spending decisions. Third, in the wake of increased spending for and attention paid to public procurement, the social and environmental impact of public procurement has gained increasing attention. This chapter is concerned with the last two of these implications, the growth of sustainable public procurement in an environment shaped by tight budgetary constraints.

The increased attention paid to public spending – amplified by a strong commitment to austerity or the goal of *the black zero* – has led to tight limits on spending for public bodies, also but not exclusively for public purchasing. This has major implications for public purchasing operations. Most obviously, tight budgetary frameworks limit the available budget. Given financial constraints and concerns about public spending, increased attention may be focused on the price of the purchase, even beyond the question of affordability. Yet sustainable consumption choices often come at higher costs. Promoting sustainability through strategic purchasing entails considerations to the social impact on those producing or delivering a good or service, as well as to the environmental impact of specific consumption choices (see Chapter 9). Higher environmental standards as well as higher wages and good working conditions are likely to induce higher costs. Take the example of the procurement of services such as welfare or ambulance services. Here, a large share of the overall cost for delivering these services is personnel costs. Consequently, higher wages and improved working conditions for those delivering the service will most likely result in higher costs for the service. In contrast, a low price may contribute to labour cost-cutting and is likely to influence the conditions of those delivering the service as well as the quality of the service. At the same time, the skills and behaviour of the person delivering the service also have an impact on the quality of the service (see Chapter 1). Consequently, a strong focus on the price may have negative impact on the quality of the service. Similar considerations hold true for goods. For instance, purchasing fair and ecologically produced uniforms (for example for the police or the fire service) or coffee or tea for canteens tends to come at a higher cost than buying conventionally produced items. Constraints on spending, and the search for a low price, enter into conflict with concerns about the social conditions of production and service delivery and environmental standards.

Further, including additional requirements such as procurement specific minimum wages or equality considerations increases the demands on administrative resources. To be effective these requirements do not only need to be included in the invitation for tenders and the contract. They also need to be verified and monitored, a task that falls onto the contracting authority, and raises demands for these. Resource constraints are important factors for the implementation (see Chapter 1) of sustainable public procurement. In brief, while strong budgetary constraints and the quest to limit public spending induce cost pressures, sustainable public procurement practices are likely to inflict higher costs and demands on resources. Consequently, sustainable public procurement recreates the tension between economic (financial), social and environmental aspects. More specifically, it is characterised by an underlying tension between cost considerations on the one hand and environmental and/or social aspects on the other. The higher the increased demands on resources (financial as well as regarding knowledge and time) and the more pronounced the constraints of resources, the more intense these tensions will be. Different approaches have been devised to facilitate sustainable public procurement.

Trends and developments

Before exploring trends and developments around sustainable public procurement, it is important to first examine developments in the broader context of sustainability. Given the increasing awareness of the social and, in particular, the environmental impact of economic development, academic research, public debate and activism have increasingly argued for revisiting economic theory and practice, for instance through the idea of **degrowth** or the **circular economy** (see Chapter 9 for information on the circular economy). Taking the economic paradigm of growth as a starting point, degrowth highlights the social (human) and environmental costs of pursuing constant and infinite growth and of measuring prosperity and development by economic growth (only). Against this background, degrowth presents a critique of the pursuit of growth regardless of the human and environmental costs, and advocates for an economy (and a society) that prioritises human and environmental wellbeing over economic growth and profit.

Indigenous knowledge can be an important source of knowledge and inspiration (see Chapter 9). Acknowledging and exploring the positive sustainability impact of and learning from Indigenous knowledge and practices can provide important inputs for more sustainable practices. In countries with a history of disregarding Indigenous populations, cultures and knowledges, engaging with Indigenous communities and First Nations may provide a way to improve (Western) practices in two ways. Firstly, by gaining insights into the needs of Indigenous communities and, secondly, by learning from them. Indigenous knowledge can be an important source of knowledge for designing more sustainable buildings, services and goods (see Chapter 9) and can thereby promote an improved sustainability impact. At the same time, engaging with Indigenous communities and involving them in the development of new practices can also benefit the communities themselves (see Box 7.2).

> **Box 7.2:** Cultural burning as sustainable practice
>
> Wildfires, particularly if wide spreading, cause considerable risks and harm to fauna, flora and human lives, livelihoods and properties. In different parts of the world, from Australia to North America, Indigenous communities are guardians of extensive knowledge on the use of consciously set controlled fires to promote biodiversity and healthy vegetation and to prevent wildfires (cultural burning), oftentimes disregarded, discredited and banned for centuries. To improve outcomes in preventing, rather than containing and fighting wildfires, and to foster biodiversity, public bodies in different parts of the world increasingly tap into this Indigenous knowledge by engaging with communities and Indigenous experts of land management. Being truly sustainable, this drive to promote Indigenous land management not only prevents fires and promotes biodiversity. It also has important economic and social impacts. It reduces costs generated by fire damage and empowers Indigenous communities, strengthens individuals' and communities' sense of identity, reduces psychological distress, and contributes to improved physical health outcomes (Adlam et al, 2021; Robinson et al, 2021).

Focusing on public procurement, several smaller trends have emerged that specifically seek to foster sustainable public procurement practices. A range of factors influence the successful implementation of sustainable public procurement, from the legal and political environment and financial aspects to the organisational setting. Over the past few decades, more and more countries have adopted legal regulations that enable or require public bodies to foster sustainable public procurement. With tight public budgets on the one hand and sustainable public procurement practices incurring higher demands on financial, personnel and time resources, sustainable public procurement is characterised by an underlying tension between available resources and financial concerns on the one hand and social and environmental considerations on the other. Different ways are emerging to ease these tensions between available resources and social and environmental criteria. To minimise the increase of work for public bodies, labels and certificates are important tools, particularly when relating to environmental criteria and to Fairtrade. Further, organisational changes (see Chapter 4) can accompany and support (socially) responsible public procurement practices. As has been highlighted in this chapter, costs are an important consideration of public procurement and socially sustainable consumption choices tend to come at higher costs than traditionally produced ones. To strengthen its focus on socially sustainable public procurement and offset additional costs, the German city of Dortmund, for instance, used savings generated by a strategic reorganisation and centralisation of its purchasing activities to offset higher costs generated by buying socially responsible products.

To successfully implement sustainable public procurement practices, knowledge of and expertise in the aligning policy goals and concepts are crucial (Grandia et al, 2013). Socially responsible purchasing in particular sets high demands for knowledge. To promote decent working and living conditions in the Global South, for instance, public procurement professionals require sound knowledge of the risks in supply chains, which need to be addressed, and ways to mitigate these risks. To promote equality (see Chapter 8), public officials carrying out public procurement procedures need to understand how inequality is perpetuated and how it can be addressed (Sarter, forthcoming). Given the importance of knowledge and expertise, several countries have established dedicated organisations that provide guidance and support for those in charge of implementing and conducting public procurement practices. In Germany, for instance, the Procurement Agency of the Federal Ministry of the Interior established the Competence Centre for Sustainable Procurement (Kompetenzstelle für nachhaltige Beschaffung), which focuses on environmental issues, and the Service Agency Communities in One World (Servicestelle Kommunen in der Einen Welt), which focuses on improving living and working conditions in the Global South; both provide guidance for public procurement. A particularly well-established centre that supports sustainable public procurement in its broadest sense is the Dutch Public Procurement Expertise Centre, PIANOo (see Box 7.3).

> **Box 7.3:** Supporting sustainable practices: the Dutch Public Procurement Expertise Centre, PIANOo
>
> In the Netherlands, the drive towards socially responsible and sustainable public procurement was supported by the establishment of the Dutch Public Procurement Expertise Centre, PIANOo (Professioneel en Innovatief Aanbesteden, Netwerk voor Overheidsopdrachtgevers [Professional and Innovative Tendering, Network for Government Contracting Authorities]). Founded in 2005, PIANOo has become an important resource for Dutch public procurement. It disseminates knowledge via publications, training and a regular newsletter, and facilitates discussions and exchange between public procurement professionals and stakeholders through meetings, conferences and a (virtual) discussion platform. PIANOo's website is an essential tool for in-depth information on public procurement, including but not limited to green or environmentally friendly procurement, circular procurement, and the promotion of international labour standards in global supply chains (*social conditions*). It contains links to tools, such as a risk checker which procurement professionals can use to assess risks in the supply chains of goods they seek to purchase, and invites specific queries, which enable access to targeted information and guidance. Providing public procurement professionals with guidance and advice, PIANOo facilitates and supports sustainable public procurement practices.

Internal support from management and an organisational culture that embraces change (see Chapters 4 and 5) are important features that facilitate a transition to (more) sustainable public procurement (Grandia et al, 2013). To promote social public procurement internally, several organisations, including but not limited to the Welsh Future Generations Commissioner, promote the appointment of **social value champions**, who advocate for (more) sustainable public procurement practices. Appointing social value champions can increase awareness, promote good practice and raise the profile of individuals committed to fostering more sustainable practices. In addition, the existence of incentive structures, which promote and reward sustainable practices, can incentivise public procurement professionals to foster sustainable practices.

Summary

While people all over the world have aimed to live in balance with nature and to mitigate human impact on the environment for centuries, sustainability as a term and a concept first emerged in Western thought in the early 18th century. Originally limited to environmental considerations, over time sustainability has expanded its scope and is today commonly understood as a three-dimensional concept, encompassing economic, social and environmental aspects. Balancing the three dimensions of sustainability poses challenges, resulting most importantly from conflicts between these dimensions.

Over the past few decades, supranational organisations have increasingly advocated sustainability. National and subnational policies increasingly incorporate sustainability as a policy goal and an overarching principle. One area, which has been a particular focus of this drive towards sustainability and is of major importance for public services, is public procurement (the purchase of works, goods and services by public bodies). The importance of public procurement for public services is twofold. For a range of public services, such as the police, who buy goods like uniforms, public procurement is an important activity to safeguard that the needs of the organisation are met. At the same time, for public services, which are contracted, public procurement has a major impact in shaping both their work and their working conditions. While public procurement increasingly must meet sustainability requirements and is placed at the heart of a growing drive towards sustainability, it is at the same time placed within a context of limited resources. Under these conditions, conflicts between the economic, the social and the environmental dimensions of sustainability gain importance.

To promote sustainability, different approaches exist. Against the backdrop of existing Indigenous knowledge and traditional sustainable practices, exploring and (re)connecting to traditional practices is gaining importance. This leads to a reconfiguration of public services' practices and is an important aspect in improving their sustainability impact. In addition to revisiting objects and practices, further approaches to support sustainable public procurement in particular aim to identify good practices, promote awareness, facilitate access to information and revisit organisational structures.

Key points

- Sustainability is a multidimensional concept, encompassing economic, social and environmental considerations.
- Conflicts between the three dimensions are common.
- Public procurement is an area in which sustainability has become increasingly important.
- A core challenge for sustainable public procurement is the tension between required and available resources, particularly in terms of financial and personnel resources and expertise.

Questions

- Why is sustainability a *Western concept*?
- What challenges are likely to arise for sustainability in practice?
- Why has public procurement received particular attention for promoting sustainability?
- Why are principal-agent problems likely to occur in public procurement?

Further reading

Bovis, C. (ed.) (2016) *Research handbook on EU public procurement law*, Cheltenham: Edward Elgar. *This book explores public procurement law in the EU, including but not limited to sustainability.*

Du Pisani, J.A. (2006) 'Sustainable development: Historical roots of the concept', *Environmental Sciences*, 3(2): 83–96. *This article examines the concept of sustainability and traces its development.*

Puvis, B., Mao, Y. and Robinson, D. (2019) 'Three pillars of sustainability: In search of conceptual origins', *Sustainability Science*, 14: 681–695. *This article explores the concept of sustainability and its origins.*

References

Adlam, C., Almendariz, D., Goode, R.W., Martinez, D.J. and Middleton, B.R. (2021) 'Keepers of the flame: Supporting the revitalization of indigenous cultural burning', *Society & Natural Resources*, available at: https://www.tandfonline.com/doi/full/10.1080/08941920.2021.2006385 [Accessed 24 January 2022].

Gailmard, S. (2014) 'Accountability and principal-agent models', in Bovens, M., Goodin, R.E. and Schillemans, T. (eds), *Oxford handbook of public accountability*, Oxford: Oxford University Press, pp 90–105.

Grandia, J., Groeneveld, S., Kuipers, B. and Steijn, B. (2013) 'Sustainable procurement in practice: Explaining the degree of sustainable procurement from an organisational perspective', *Rivista di Politica Economica*, 2: 41–66.

Hannes, S. (2007) 'Reverse monitoring: On the hidden role of employee stock-based compensation', *Michigan Law Review*, 10597: 1438–1439.

Hardin, G. (1968) 'The tragedy of the commons', *Science*, 162: 1243–1248.

Mazzocchi, F. (2020) 'A deeper meaning of sustainability: Insights from indigenous knowledge', *The Anthropocene Review*, 7(1): 77–93.

OECD (2019) *Government at a glance 2019*, Paris: OECD Publishing, available at: https://doi.org/10.1787/8ccf5c38-en [Accessed 24 January 2022].

Ostrom, E. (1990) *Governing the commons: The evolution of institutions for collective action*, Cambridge: Cambridge University Press.

Ostrom, E. (2000) 'Collective action and the evolution of social norms', *Journal of Economic Perspectives*, 14(3): 137–158.

Pollitt, C. and Bouckaert, G. (2011) *Public management reform: A comparative analysis: New public management, governance, and the neo-Weberian state*, Oxford: Oxford University Press.

Robinson, C.J., Costello, O., Lockwood, M., Pert, P.L. and Garnett, S.T. (2021) *Empowering indigenous leadership and participation in bushfire recovery, cultural burning and land management*, NESP Threatened Species Recovery Hub Project 8.2.1 Technical report, Brisbane, available at: https://www.nespthreatenedspecies.edu.au/media/bs4abb5v/8-2-1-empowering-indigenous-leadership-and-participation-in-bushfire-recovery-cultural-burning-and-land-management-report_v6.pdf [Accessed 24 January 2022].

Sarter, E.K. (2015) 'The legal framework of contracting: Gender equality, the provision of services, and European public procurement law', *Wagadu: A Transnational Journal of Women's and Gender Studies*, 14: 55–83, available at: https://bit.ly/3ouWgY7 [Accessed 24 January 2022].

Sarter, E.K. (forthcoming) 'The challenge of knowing: Public procurement between unilateral knowledge dissemination and participatory knowledge creation', in Nyeck, S.N. (ed.), *Gender, vulnerability theory and public procurement: Perspectives on global reform*, New York: Routledge.

Sarter, E.K. and Karamanidou, L. (2019) 'Quality, qualifications, and the market: Procuring interpretation services in the context of the "refugee crisis"', *Social Policy & Administration*, 53(3): 493–507.

Steurer, R., Martinuzzi, A. and Margula, S. (2012) 'Public policies on CSR in Europe: Themes, instruments, and regional differences', *Corporate Social Responsibility and Environment Management*, 19(4): 206–227.

UN (1997) *Agenda for development. Resolution adopted by the General Assembly. 51/240*, available at: http://undocs.org/en/A/RES/51/240 [Accessed 24 January 2022].

UN (2011) *Guiding principles on business and human rights: Implementing the United Nations 'protect, respect and remedy' framework*, New York and Geneva: United Nations Human Rights Office of the High Commissioner.

Welsh Government (2016) *Shared purpose: Shared future. Statutory guidance on the Well-being of Future Generations (Wales) Act 2015*, available at: https://gov.wales/sites/default/files/publications/2019-02/spsf-1-core-guidance.PDF [Accessed 24 January 2022].

World Commission on Environment and Development (1987) *Report of the World Commission on Environment and Development: Our common future*, available at: http://www.un-documents.net/wced-ocf.htm [Accessed 24 January 2022].

8

Public services and equality

E.K. Sarter, Wendy Booth and Vida Greaux

Chapter objectives

Over the past decades, equality has become an increasingly important concern. Since the mid-20th century, a growing number of legal regulations aim to abolish discrimination and promote equality. This chapter shows that while equality has gained increasing importance over the past few decades, inequalities persist. Starting first with the distinction between equality of outcome and equality of opportunity, and secondly between formal and substantial equality, this chapter highlights that different understandings of the term equality exist, and points to the importance of acknowledging the nature and root of inequalities (as issues of redistribution or recognition) for identifying how specific inequalities can best be addressed. Equality can refer to equality between groups, which are constructed based on one shared feature, or take an intersectional perspective, aiming to address the multifaceted and complex nature of inequality. Turning to public services and their linkage to equality, this chapter highlights the importance of considering also (implicit) access requirements, the service and the conditions under which it is delivered, and outlines key strategies public services are using to promote equality both externally and internally.

Introduction

Over the past few decades, equality considerations have gained growing policy prominence. Since the middle of the 20th century, an increasing number of public policies and legal regulations in different countries have aimed to counteract discrimination and foster equality. Promoting equality remains a core concern of policies because, despite the growing importance of promoting equality, inequalities persist. For instance, public transport in Wales has been shown to neglect the specific needs of people with disabilities (Equality and Human Rights Commission, 2020). Deaf people in Wales face barriers when using healthcare services (Terry et al, 2021). The likelihood of being physically restrained while in police custody in England and Wales is considerably higher for ethnic minorities than for White individuals (Equality and Human Rights Commission, 2016: 9);

Black African women in England face a seven times higher risk of being detained under mental health law than their White British counterparts (Equality and Human Rights Commission, 2016: 8).

Equality is a core consideration for public services for several reasons. First, fostering equality may be considered a **normative obligation**. This means that equality can be comprehended as a value in and of itself that should be promoted for moral and ethical reasons. The degree to which this is the case differs according to values, norms and dominant political positions (see Introduction and Chapter 1). Second, legal obligations may require public services to operate in a non-discriminatory way and promote equality. Within the European Union (EU), for instance, European law (see Chapter 3) sets out equality requirements, including regulations that explicitly refer to the provision of services, such as *Council Directive 2004/113/EC of 13 December 2004 implementing the principle of equal treatment between men and women in the access to and supply of goods and services.* A third argument for the importance of considering (in)equalities derives from the function of public services to address service user needs and protect citizen rights including civil rights (see Introduction), combined with the fact that different lived experiences lead to diverging needs and requirements. Differences between individuals, their situations and experiences mean that needs and the use of, the access to and the impact of services differ. Consequently, not accounting for different needs and requirements may decrease the effectiveness of public services in reaching their goals. Focusing on gender equality specifically, a similar argument has been prominently made by Himmelweit (2002) regarding public policies. Across the world, women are more likely to engage in unpaid work, such as household chores or care work, than men. In Japan, women spent on average 224.3 minutes per day in unpaid and 271.5 minutes in paid work compared to 40.8 minutes in unpaid and 451.8 minutes in paid work for men. While the overall difference varies between countries, the same picture emerges across the world. In Denmark, for instance, men spent a considerably higher amount of time doing unpaid work; however, women still spent on average 242.8 minutes per day on unpaid work and men 186.1 minutes. In contrast, men spend more time in paid employment (260.1 minutes) than women (194.6 minutes) (OECD, 2021). If policies neglect this difference, it may result in a situation where a policy based on the situation of one group of people (those without major engagement in the unpaid economy) is applied to individuals in a significantly different situation (here, those with major involvement in the unpaid economy). Against this backdrop, Himmelweit argues that this 'policy will be badly targeted and therefore, at worst, ineffective in achieving its goals' (Himmelweit, 2002: 51). As public services serve a diverse population, a similar argument can be made here. If public services do not account for the differing needs that go along with this diverse population, they may fail to successfully and effectively address the needs of parts of the population, and consequently fail to meet their aims.

In addition to a focus on the users, this chapter argues that equality within public services is an important consideration. Neglecting equality within the workforce can lead to decreased motivation and productivity (Badal and Harter, 2014), less engagement (Ellison and Mullin, 2014) and increased turnover of staff; features that can significantly affect the service and its impact on users.

This chapter explores equality with a particular focus on public services. It first outlines different approaches to understanding equality. This chapter then turns to examine the relationship between public services and equality before highlighting trends and developments relating to public services and equality.

Considering equality

While equality is a widely used term which forms part of everyday language, different interpretations of the term exist. Therefore, it is essential to consider the term **equality** itself before turning to the linkage between equality and public services.

A first important distinction is the difference between **equality of outcome** and **equality of opportunity** (Platt, 2019: 236–241). **Equality of outcome** aims to equalise results; it focuses on real-life outcomes – the actual situation that different people find themselves in. As disadvantages result from circumstances beyond an individual's control (for instance, from circumstances people grew up in and different opportunities in earlier life or social prejudices and biases), equality of outcome aims to mitigate the impact of unequal structures. Approaches based on a vision of equality of outcome take active steps to mitigate these differences, for instance through redistribution of resources. In contrast, **equality of opportunity** aims to promote equality by fostering equal chances for individuals. In its minimum version, equal opportunities may be taken to mean non-discrimination only. It may, however, also be interpreted as promoting equal chances through measures to mitigate (pre-)existing disadvantages. While in practice equality of opportunity and equality of outcome may be linked, it is important to acknowledge these two distinct approaches as they provide different lenses to understand equality as a goal.

Another important distinction is that between **formal** and **substantial** equality. **Formal equality** focuses on ensuring fairness by always treating everyone equally. In contrast, **substantive equality** acknowledges differences among people and their varying needs and options. Taken in this sense, formal equality can have very different implications for people in different situations. This was most pointedly stated by the French writer Anatole France, who has been attributed as saying: 'The law, in its majestic equality, forbids all men to sleep under bridges, to beg in the streets and to steal bread – the rich as well as the poor.' Here, rich and poor are formally equal (neither rich nor poor people are allowed to sleep under bridges, beg in the streets or steal bread). However, while formally equal, rich and poor people are very differently affected by this regulation as rich people have recourse to houses, money and food, while the poorest lack these resources. With a lack of sheltered places to sleep, money or food, poor (homeless) people may have to take recourse to sleeping under bridges, begging or stealing bread (to survive).

An approach that is increasingly used in practice is the **capability approach**. It provides a normative framework for assessing wellbeing, social arrangements, policies and plans or ideas for future developments. The starting point for the capability approach is different needs and the substantive freedom to make choices about things that matter to an individual. The fundamental idea of the capability approach is that the objective of justice 'should be to expand the freedom that deprived people have to enjoy "valuable beings and doings". They should have access to the necessary positive resources, and they should be able to make choices that matter to them'(Alkire, 2005: 117). Societal arrangements should provide individuals with the necessary resources to have the substantial freedom to make these choices.

In brief, equality can be understood in different ways; it can focus on formal equal treatment of everyone, aim to reduce inequality of real-life outcomes or focus on providing everyone with the opportunity to make choices that are important to them. How equality is perceived by a specific organisation, institution or individual depends on their specific background, culture and values.

To effectively address inequalities, it is crucial to identify their nature. Fraser (1995) proposes to distinguish between those inequalities that result from the socioeconomic structure and those whose origin lies in culture, which are 'rooted in social patterns of representation, interpretation, and communication' (Fraser, 1995: 71). Some categories linked to equality, such as class, are linked to socioeconomic conditions and can be addressed by **redistribution**. Other aspects, such as sexual orientation, are better understood as linked to culture, as an issue of **recognition**. While socioeconomically founded inequality can be addressed (and equality promoted) by redistributing resources, issues of recognition require a different approach. For issues of recognition, which are rooted in social patterns and interpretations, redistribution of resources will not have a significant impact. Cultural and social change is needed to improve equality. Other aspects, such as gender or race, encompass aspects of recognition and redistribution. These issues that combine aspects of redistribution and recognition require a combined approach.

Equality for whom?

When considering the equality impact of public services, it is a question not only of what equality means but also of for whom equality is sought. Often, when inequalities are considered and equality is promoted, there is a distinct focus on certain groups based on a shared characteristic. It is assumed that this characteristic impacts on lives and lived experiences. For example, policies and measures could focus on promoting equality between men and women, White and Black individuals, Deaf and hearing people, and so on. The British Public Sector Equality Duty, which forms part of the Equality Act 2010, and outlines a legal requirement for public bodies to promote equality, for instance, focuses on a set of protected characteristics, namely age, disability, gender reassignment, pregnancy and maternity, race, religion or belief, sex, and sexual orientation.

When considering **group-based approaches** to equality, it is important to acknowledge that the groups in question are **socially constructed**, and that this construction is dependent on the meaning given to particular characteristics. Especially in the context of policies promoting equality, groups are generally based on specific features that shape structures. To visualise this, take the example of the size of one's feet and the colour of one's skin. Having big or small feet is seen as an individual yet not a socially important feature. In general, it affects lived experiences only in a very limited number of situations, such as when buying socks or shoes. In contrast, the colour of one's skin has socially and historically been constructed as having an important meaning. Consequently, the colour of one's skin has an important impact on one's lived experience.

As the importance attached to a specific feature is socially constructed, its importance may vary over time and space. Perhaps the most obvious example of this is the history of what in Anglo-Saxon contexts is often referred to as 'race'. In this context, it seems important to acknowledge the cultural differences in terms used to describe and identify specific groups (see Box 8.1).

In several countries, from the US to South Africa (under Apartheid), 'race' was historically the basis for separate regulations and rules and the legal discrimination of Black people and People of Colour. While important substantial inequalities persist, nowadays legal regulations ensure formal equality. Likewise, the importance of other categories, such as sex or sexual orientation, varies across countries and has seen important shifts in many places.

Box 8.1: Terminology matters

Words and terminologies are important parts of creating an inclusive environment, combating discrimination and prejudice, and promoting equality. Words used to refer to features upon which discrimination can be based, and to groups of people, can change over time and differ between countries. While the term 'race', for instance, is commonly used in some countries, such as the UK, it is seen as contentious in others. In Germany, for example, the equivalent of this term is not used in contemporary language. Recent years have seen important debates about the persistence of the term in German laws that prohibit racist discrimination. Institutions such as the German Institute for Human Rights (Deutsches Institut für Menschenrechte) have pointed to the fact that using the term 'race' suggests that different human races exist. This, however, is a scientifically disproven fact and the basis for racist ideologies. Using the term therefore promotes ideas (the existence of more than one human race) that lay the ground for racist worldviews. Consequently, the German Institute for Human Rights argued that ceasing to use the term in legal documents was an important part of countering racist worldviews. Further, by using this term as a characteristic for non-discrimination policies, it highlighted, those wanting to make complaints about racist discrimination are forced to use inherently racist terminology (Cremer, 2020).

Yet it is not only the importance attached to specific characteristics that varies. Being socially constructed, the definition of categories and groups may vary across time and space. Take the example of sex, which was (in legal and official terms) initially a dichotomous category in Germany. Following a ruling issued by Germany's Constitutional Court (*Bundesverfassungsgericht*), Germany introduced the legal recognition of an official third sex (*diverse*) in addition to the previously existing options of *male* and *female*. Further, how belonging to a specific group is determined may vary. In the case of officially recorded sex, for instance, it can be based on medical/anatomical grounds or self-identification. In brief, the question of how many and which groups are constructed, and how belonging to a specific group is attributed, is a social construction, which is reflected in social and legal norms and can vary between locations.

Group-based approaches inevitably spring from generalisations and inherently assume that individuals who share a common characteristic are positioned in a similar way. This has, however, led to criticism of the underlying assumption that individuals who share one characteristic find themselves in a similar position. Rather than finding themselves in a similar position, it has been argued, individuals who share one particular characteristic (such as sex) may be in a very different position due to other characteristics. Different characteristics overlap and interact, positioning individuals very differently. In other words, White women's experiences differ from those of Black women. Straight ciswomen have different lived experiences than lesbian transwomen, and so on. Group-based approaches have been argued to neglect the vast heterogeneity within a defined group, running the risk of oversimplifying reality. Thereby, they are likely to fail to account for the experiences of those members of a group, who face disadvantages from different sources. In the example of *women*, this would mean basing an understanding of the group on the experiences of White middle-class cisgender women while neglecting the experiences of Black-working class transwomen. As Crenshaw (1989: 140) pointed out, the 'focus on the most privileged group members marginalizes those who are multiply-burdened, and obscures claims that cannot be understood as resulting from discrete sources of discrimination'. As a result of these criticisms, the concept of intersectionality (Crenshaw, 1989; 1991) has gained prominence. **Intersectionality** aims to transcend the boundaries erected by group-based approaches and seeks a nuanced understanding of the multilayered nature of inequality, which results from the intersection of different features. It highlights the importance of the individual combination of characteristics and their interaction when considering (in)equality.

Equality and public services

Public services are important actors, who shape policy outcomes (see Chapter 1) and social and societal (in)equality. They can reduce or reinforce inequalities.

Various features come together to form the equality impact of services, beginning with the initial need that public services respond to.

Public services are established to respond to specific needs (see Introduction), which have been politically assessed as warranting public attention. As with policies, where the problems identified and addressed have important implications for their impact (see Chapter 1), so does the definition of essential needs shape the impact of the services that are delivered. Without going into detail, it is vital to acknowledge that at a very basic level, the assessment of which needs warrant public attention (and which do not) can have important implications for equality. To understand this, take the example of childcare services. They are of particular importance to primary carers, the majority of whom are women. Childcare services, especially those that are publicly funded and delivered free of charge to everyone at the point of use (for instance, in the case of the French *école maternelle*), enable all primary carers to choose between devoting their time to childcare and engaging in other tasks, such as paid employment. Childcare services increase opportunities for carers to generate an individual income, and decrease their dependence on, for instance, a partner's income, savings or benefits. Without free or affordable childcare options, carers may find themselves either dependent on social networks or savings, or without a choice of whether to engage in other activities and/or care for someone. As primary carers are in most cases women, the question of whether childcare is publicly provided (and at what cost) has important consequences not only for individual options and opportunities but also for gender equality at a broader level.

Further, taking account of different lived experiences and living situations is crucial when considering (implicit) **access** requirements of existing public services. Expanding the example of caring responsibilities: if a specific service is only accessible to those who are (at the time that they need the service) without immediate caring responsibilities, individuals with caring responsibilities may be precluded from using the service. If, for example, a refugee with caring responsibilities wants to access a language course for refugees but can neither access childcare nor bring their children with them, they may be precluded from using this service altogether, which may in turn affect their integration (Cheung and Phillimore, 2017). Given that primary carers are in their majority women, female refugees with caring responsibilities may experience disadvantage not only in relation to non-refugees but also in relation to male and female refugees without caring responsibilities. Likewise, language requirements and a lack of services in alternative languages, such as sign language, and/or a lack of adequate interpretation may effectively pose a barrier to using services for individuals whose native language is not the (main) languagage of the country they reside in (migrants or linguistic minorities) (see Box 8.2).

Further, how public services are delivered can have important implications. The actions and behaviour of street-level bureaucrats (those working in public service roles, where they have direct interaction with citizens and hold discretion [Lipsky, 1980]) are especially important for shaping policy outcomes (see Chapter 1) and the equality impact of services (Sarter and Benjamin, forthcoming). The skills and competencies of the person delivering the service and the way they treat the user shape the impact of the service as well as the experiences of its users. The necessary skills and competencies are not limited to professional knowledge. They also encompass personal and communication skills. Particularly in **person-centred** (or **soft**) services (such as social services or education), caring skills, empathy and the ability to form trusting relationships with users are essential (Sarter and Karamanidou, 2019). These are necessary components for delivering a positively impactful (soft) service and particularly crucial when delivering public services to, or dealing with, vulnerable individuals or members of marginalised communities. An existing and/or perceived lack of awareness, understanding, relationship building skills and empathy can have important implications for the service and its users. For instance, research on mental health services has highlighted a lack of awareness of the lived experiences of Black and ethnic minority service users, which resulted in providers being perceived as 'unresponsive to the needs of ethnic minority groups' (Memon et al, 2016: 7). This was found to reinforce perceptions and experiences of racism, discrimination and exclusion on the side of Black and ethnic minority users (Memon et al, 2016: 7), and to affect the impact of the services themselves. To fully capture the equality impact of public services, it is crucial to consider how they affect different users as well as broader societal equality.

> **Box 8.2:** Accessing public services
>
> In Wales, only a limited number of specific health services for Deaf people exist. This means that Deaf people need to use services designed for the hearing community. To enable these services to be effective means ensuring that meaningful communication is possible. At the very least, interpreting needs to warrant that meaningful communication can take place. However, when considering the practice, forms for new patients in the UK hardly enquire about hearing, which means that specific requirements for interpreting are not recorded. Further, it has been shown that general healthcare practitioners in the UK often have no knowledge of how to arrange for British Sign Language (BSL) interpreters to be present at appointments. Consequently, Deaf patients have to actively ask or arrange for interpreters to be present to ensure meaningful communication is possible in healthcare settings. However, as patients, Deaf people and people with hearing loss may not be aware of the arrangements for BSL interpretation. Coupled with a lack of BSL interpreters in the UK, these arrangements may pose significant barriers for Deaf people when accessing and using health services (Terry et al, 2021). As a result, 'access to health services is a major problem' for Deaf people in Wales (Terry et al, 2021: 4).

To gain a holistic picture of equality and public services, it is insufficient to only consider the services, their design and how they are delivered. Public service organisations are themselves institutions and employers, which can promote equality or be shaped by inequality. To fully understand the relationship between public services and equality, consideration of how far public services are characterised by (in)equality within and for their workforce is crucial. Take the example of higher education in the UK. The curriculum and the (in)visibility of specific groups have important impacts for students. However, they are by far not the only aspects relating to equality. While the share of Black and ethnic minority students may have increased significantly, research highlights persisting inequalities within higher education. Black academics and academics from ethnic minority communities face obstacles, discrimination and difficulties when accessing the labour market, securing permanent positions and applying for promotions. Wage gaps linked to ethnicity persist and individuals from Black and ethnic communities remain underrepresented, particularly in senior roles and positions with decision-making powers (Arday, 2018; Bhopal, 2020). Workplaces and organisational cultures (see Chapter 4) display a lack of awareness and action regarding the challenges faced by Black academics and academics from ethnic minority backgrounds. In the face of a lack of awareness and of organisational cultures that perpetuate inequality, 'disruption of these inequitable cultures for BME [Black and ethnic minority] staff can leave residual effects which affect self-esteem and leave BME staff open to claims of hypersensitivity or trouble-making when challenging racism' (Arday, 2018: 193). Unequal treatment, opportunities and, ultimately, workplaces do not only result from blatant conscious racism but may be induced by **unconscious bias**, that is, stereotypes and prejudices that reside outside an individual's conscious awareness. Unconscious biases not only influence individual perceptions but can also contribute to an organisational culture that creates and/or perpetuates inequality.

As already mentioned, for person–centred services, the service and the person delivering it are intrinsically linked. In addition to the obvious implications that unequal workplaces have for staff, by virtue of their impact on the person delivering a service, inequality and unequal treatment of staff in public services can also affect service users (see Chapter 1). Workplace cultures that affect the wellbeing and mental health of those delivering a service can affect the way in which the person delivers a service, which affects the service, its quality and the user. Considering the linkage between public services and equality therefore also requires considering public services as workplaces and the impact that the state of equality within a service has for its users.

Trends and developments

Public services and public sector organisations are adopting a range of different measures to promote equality, both internally and externally. To foster a deep(er) understanding of equality and the promotion of equality, public sector organisations and public services provide **training** for staff around the legal and institutional requirements or through unconscious bias training. Further, **equality**

impact assessments are an important tool for assessing the impact that a specific course of action has for equality.

Community engagement and **co-production** are increasingly used to better consider the needs and concerns of different public service users. To identify the impact of services and to better understand the needs of different users, the concept of co-production is gaining increasing attention in public services (see Chapter 4). Co-production aims to bring 'public services, service users and communities' together with the aim of 'making better use of each other's assets and resources to achieve better outcomes or improved efficiency' (Loeffler and Bovaird, 2016: 1006). Co-production can take different forms, such as communities and their members contributing to public inquiries or focus groups, which may lead to changes in public service delivery. To gain a holistic understanding of the impact of a distinct public service, it is essential to include a broad range of users, who can shed light on the intersectional impact of a specific service.

In the search for effective means to promote equality, the purchasing of goods, works and services by public bodies, **public procurement** (see Chapter 7), is gaining increasing importance (see Box 8.3). Based on the high amount that public bodies spend on the purchase of goods, construction works and services, public policies, for instance in Scotland, increasingly couple public procurement with equality considerations (Sarter and Thomson, 2020).

Box 8.3: Promoting equality in healthcare

In the UK, a gap exists between the life expectancy of men and that of women. Aiming to reduce the gap in life expectancy, a health organisation in the UK focused on the unequal likelihood of visiting a General Practitioner (GP). Single men (and particularly single gay men) over 50 in the UK are less likely to consult their GP than women. To increase the likelihood that older single, and particularly gay, men consulted their GP, the health organisation made use of their public contracts. In the **invitation for tender**, which it issued for a contract for community health communication, the health organisation required those bidding for a contract to outline a plan on how to improve GP consultations of single older, and particularly gay, men. The successful bidder proposed the promotion of health information and advice to consult GPs via posters and beer mats distributed in local pubs frequented by the target audience. Following this project, consultation rates of single, older, gay men visiting GPs increased (Equality and Human Rights Commission Scotland, 2013: 19).

To foster equality internally, public sector organisations and services have also looked at recruitment practices. Given that applicants from an ethnic minority have unequal chances of being invited to an interview, public (and private) employers have, over the past decade, initiated small- and large-scale (pilot) projects to test **anonymous** or **name–blind recruitment processes**. In these, the available information in the initial stage does not include identifying factors such as the name of the applicant. Some of these have been evaluated rigorously; they seem to suggest that name-blind applications lead to higher rates of invitation for interviews by minority candidates. It is, however, important to note that higher rates of being invited to an interview did not necessarily translate into higher offer rates for minority candidates (Rinne, 2018).

Summary

Equality is an important issue for public services. In addition to moral considerations and legal obligations, equality is crucial for public services' ability to effectively address the needs of a wide range of users. Equality can be conceptualised in different ways. It can focus on providing (more) equal opportunities or fostering (more) equal outcomes. Equality can refer to formal or substantial equality. To identify ways to promote equality it is crucial to examine the root and nature of a specific inequality to determine the best way of addressing it; more specifically, it is important to understand whether a given inequality is an issue of redistribution or recognition. Lastly, the capability approach provides a normative framework for enabling individuals to enjoy the freedom to make choices about their lives. However, it is not only important to scrutinise the concept of equality. The question is also how to assess equality and how to envision inequality within a context, where a wide range of aspects may impact an individual's situation. Group-based approaches focus on assessing and improving the situation for a specific group, whose definition relies on members sharing *one* common (socially constructed) feature that shapes structures and individual lives; they tend to generalise the experiences of people sharing this characteristic. This may lead to a focus on the more privileged members of a group at the cost of neglecting the experiences of people living at the intersection of different features that give rise to disadvantage. Against this background, intersectionality aims to account for the complexity of the world and the multifaceted nature of inequality.

Whether and how public services account for differences and take equality into account has important implications. Of particular importance in this context is firstly which needs public services address; secondly, whether and how they consider (whose) needs; thirdly, how access requirements interact with the lived experiences of a wide range of different users; and fourthly, how the service is delivered. At the same time, public services are also workplaces. Considering equality in relation to public services also means examining practices within public services themselves. This holds particularly true as unequal workplaces have important implications for those working in them, for the organisation and the service, thereby also affecting service users. In addition to providing training for those working in public services, co-production of services is increasingly gaining importance as one way to better align public service provision with the needs of diverse users.

Key points

- Different interpretations of equality exist.
- Inequality can be rooted in socioeconomic patterns, cultural patterns, or both.
- Equality considerations can focus on socially constructed groups, which share a common feature, or take an intersectional perspective.
- The equality impact of a public service depends on access requirements, the design of the service, and the way it is delivered.
- Equality within the workforce can have a significant impact on the service and its users.

Questions

- What is the difference between formal and substantial equality?
- Why are groups socially constructed and what does that mean?
- Which factors shape the equality impact of public services?
- Why do the skills, competencies and working conditions of those delivering a public service matter for the service user?

Further reading

Lister, R. (2014) 'The importance of equality', in Hatterley, R. and Hickson, K. (eds), *Social democracy in contemporary Britain*, London: IB Tauris. *This book examines equality as the focal point of policy and politics.*

White, S. (2007) *Equality*, Cambridge: Polity Press. *This book explores key issues related to (in)equality, from democracy, the role of the state and the social contract, to key points of contention.*

References

Alkire, S. (2005) 'Why the capability approach?', *Journal of Human Development*, 6(1): 115–133.

Arday, J. (2018) 'Understanding race and educational leadership in higher education: Exploring the Black and ethnic minority (BME) experience', *Management in Education*, 32(4): 192–200.

Badal, S. and Harter, J.K. (2014) 'Gender diversity, business-unit engagement, and performance', *Journal of Leadership & Organizational Studies*, 21(4): 354–365.

Bhopal, K. (2020) 'Gender, ethnicity and career progression in UK higher education: A case study analysis', *Research Papers in Education*, 35(6): 706–721.

Cheung, S.Y. and Phillimore, J. (2017) 'Gender and refugee integration: A quantitative analysis of integration and social policy outcomes', *Journal of Social Policy*, 46(2): 211–230.

Council Directive 2004/113/EC of 13 December 2004 implementing the principle of equal treatment between men and women in the access to and supply of goods and services. OJL 373, 21.12.2004: 37–43.

Cremer, H. (2020) *Das Verbot rassistischer Diskriminierung. Vorschlag für eine Änderung von Artikel 3 Absatz 3 Satz 1 Grundgesetz*, Berlin: Deutsches Institut für Menschenrechte, available at: https://www.institut-fuer-menschenrechte. de/fileadmin/Redaktion/Publikationen/Analyse_Studie/Analyse_Verbot_ra ssistischer_Diskriminierung.pdf [Accessed 23 January 2022].

Crenshaw, K. (1989) 'Demarginalizing the intersection of race and sex: A black feminist critique of antidiscrimination doctrine, feminist theory and antiracist politics', *University of Chicago Legal Forum*, 1: Article 8, available at: http://chi cagounbound.uchicago.edu/uclf/vol1989/iss1/8 [Accessed 23 January 2022].

Crenshaw, K. (1991) 'Mapping the margins: Intersectionality, identity politics, and violence against women of color', *Stanford Law Review*, 43(6): 1241–1299.

Ellison, S.F. and Mullin, W.P. (2014) 'Diversity, social goods provision, and performance in the firm', *Journal of Economics & Management Strategy*, 23(2): 465–481.

Equality and Human Rights Commission (2016) *Healing a divided Britain: The need for a comprehensive race equality strategy*, available at: https://www.equalityhuma nrights.com/en/publication-download/healing-divided-britain-need-compre hensive-race-equality-strategy [Accessed 23 January 2022].

Equality and Human Rights Commission (2020) *Accessible public transport for older and disabled people in Wales*, available at: https://www.equalityhumanrights.com/ en/publication-download/accessible-public-transport-older-and-disabled-peo ple-wales [Accessed 23 January 2022].

Equality and Human Rights Commission Scotland (2013) *Procurement and the public sector equality duty: A guide for public authorities (Scotland)*, available at: https://www. equalityhumanrights.com/sites/default/files/ehrc_procurement_guidance_ 2013_-_final.doc [Accessed 23 January 2022].

Fraser, N. (1995) 'From redistribution to recognition? Dilemmas of justice in a "post-socialist" age', *New Left Review*, 212: 68–93.

Himmelweit, S. (2002) 'Making visible the hidden economy: The case for gender-impact analysis of economic policy', *Feminist Economics*, 8(1): 49–70.

Lipsky, M. (1980) *Street-level bureaucracy: Dilemmas of the individual in public services*, New York: Russell Sage Foundation.

Loeffler, E. and Bovaird, T. (2016) 'User and community co-production of public services: What does the evidence tell us?', *International Journal of Public Administration*, 39(13): 1006–1019.

Memon, A., Taylor, K., Mohebati, L.M., Sundin, J., Cooper, M., Scanlon, T. and de Visser, R. (2016) 'Perceived barriers to accessing mental health services among black and minority ethnic (BME) communities: A qualitative study in southeast England', *British Medical Journal Open*, 6(11): e012337, available at: https://bmjopen.bmj.com/content/bmjopen/6/11/e012337.full.pdf [Accessed 23 January 2022].

OECD (2021) *Employment: Time spent in paid and unpaid work, by sex*, available at: https://stats.oecd.org/index.aspx?queryid=54757 [Accessed 23 January 2022].

Platt, L. (2019) *Understanding inequalities: Stratification and difference*, Cambridge: Policy.

Rinne, U. (2018) 'Anonymous job applications and hiring discrimination', *IZA World of Labor* 2018: 48, available at: doi: 10.15185/izawol.48.v2 [Accessed 23 January 2022].

Sarter, E.K. and Benjamin, O. (forthcoming) 'Contrasted vulnerability? Job quality, service quality and public procurement of services', in Nyeck, S.N. (ed.), *Gender, vulnerability theory and public procurement: Perspectives on global reform*, New York: Routledge.

Sarter, E.K. and Karamanidou, L. (2019) 'Quality, qualifications, and the market: Procuring interpretation services in the context of the "refugee crisis"', *Social Policy & Administration*, 53(3): 493–507.

Sarter, E.K. and Thomson, E. (2020) 'Fulfilling its promise? Strategic public procurement and the impact of equality considerations on employers' behaviour in Scotland', *Public Money & Management*, 40(6): 437–445.

Terry, J., Redfern, P., Bond, J., Fowler-Powe, M. and Booth, C. (2021) *Deaf people Wales: Hidden inequality*, All Wales Deaf Mental Health & Well-Being Group, available at: https://www.swansea.ac.uk/media/Deaf-People-Wales_Hidden-Inequality-2021.pdf [Accessed 23 January 2022].

9

Public services and
the environmental crisis

E.K. Sarter

Chapter objectives

From the extinction of species and the loss of biodiversity to climate change, a growing scientific consensus exists that, as a direct result of human activity, the ecological systems which support life on earth are threatened with potentially irreparable and catastrophic damage. This chapter explores this **environmental crisis** and shows that it affects public services in two ways. First, it impacts the human individuals and communities that public services serve and modifies the conditions under which public services are delivered, and the circumstances of their working. Consequently, changing environmental conditions require public services to adapt. Secondly, public services themselves contribute to the environmental crisis. The delivery of public services has an environmental impact, which is shaped by the work the specific services carry out, emissions and wastage produced, and the environmental impact of resources and tools used. This chapter outlines that public services can contribute to broader attempts to mitigate the environmental crisis by limiting their environmental impact. At the same time, they can be crucial for promoting environmental knowledge and awareness and thereby support broader attempts to mitigate the environmental impact of humanity and consequently the environmental crisis.

Introduction

Public services organisations are context bound; their tasks and ways of working are shaped by their context. Environmental changes, including but not limited to increasing pollution, the extinction of species, the loss of biodiversity and climate change, are among the most important challenges of our time. The different facets of what can be labelled an environmental crisis have important implications for public services. Based on an outline of different and interrelated facets of the **environmental crisis**, this chapter explores the importance of the human impact on the planet and the key challenges the environmental crisis poses. Focusing on public services, this chapter highlights that the different facets of the environmental crisis have important implications for public services, who need to adapt. Climate change, for instance, means that extreme weather events, be they droughts or floods, are likely to occur more often and to gain in intensity. With an increasing number of extreme weather events – also in areas where they were previously less common – new or increased challenges exist for public services. Some services, such as fire services or the police, are directly involved in the response to these events, while others, such as schools or social services, may have to adapt the way they deliver their services. Air pollution increases the risk of a range of diseases, endangering human health, which can increase pressure on health services. Like climate change and pollution, the loss of biodiversity may affect public services negatively, particularly healthcare. As nature is an important source for the development of medication, the loss of biodiversity may, for example, limit the potential to develop new drugs, affecting health services' ability to treat illnesses (Díaz et al, 2019).

Yet, as this chapter shows, the relationship between public services and the environment is not limited to the emergence of new challenges to which public services must adapt. Public services themselves have an environmental impact, an ecological footprint. To function effectively, public services may, for instance, use vehicles and/or electronic appliances (for example computers); they require heating for offices and other buildings. All of this has an environmental impact. In addition, tools, vehicles and buildings used by public services need to be cleaned; this requires resources and creates wastewater. Further, public services themselves create wastage, be it in the form of paper, old IT hardware, used plastic gloves or bio-waste. This waste has an environmental impact. This chapter outlines that because public services themselves have a distinct environmental impact, they can work towards limiting their own environmental impact. Thereby, they can be part of broader approaches to mitigate the environmental crisis and act as role models for shifts towards more environmentally friendly practices. Further, this chapter argues that public services, and education services in particular, can act as multiplicators of environmental awareness and knowledge.

The environmental crisis

Before exploring the impact of the environmental crisis on public services, it is important to understand the larger context of this crisis, its key facets and its core implications for humanity. One of the most prominent aspects of the environmental crisis (if not the most prominent one) is **climate change** (see Chapter 10). It increases the likelihood of extreme weather events such as flooding, which are becoming more frequent and intense, affecting human lives and livelihoods. It also makes heatwaves more likely, which contribute to droughts and may have adverse effects for human health. Water from melting glaciers and ice sheets, alongside the expansion of warming water, contribute to rising sea levels, which pose essential risks, particularly for coastal areas and low-lying islands.

At the same time, and interlinked with these developments, a growing number of species are in danger of becoming extinct. The human impact on nature has significantly changed the face of the planet. In combination with increasing pollution and other developments, this has led to a loss of habitat, leading to more and more plants and animals facing danger of **extinction**. When applying the criteria of the Conservation of Nature's Red List, about 25 per cent of the animal and plant species of which humanity knows enough to be able to assess their status, are endangered (Díaz et al, 2019: 24). The increasing threat of extinction of species also has important implications for humans, as it may affect food security (Díaz et al, 2019: 11–26). For instance, pollinators such as insects, some of which are in danger of extinction, are a crucial part of nature without whom many plants and foods would not grow.

Pollution is a further important aspect of today's environmental crisis. Take the example of plastic pollution. Between 1950 and 2015 the total plastic production has been estimated to account for 8.3 billion metric tons; between 1950 and 2017, it has increased by an estimated 20,000 per cent. Only a small part of the total plastic produced between 1950 and 2015 has ever been recycled: it has been estimated that only one-third of the total 8.3 billion metric tons produced between 1950 and 2015 is still in use, and only 600 million metric tons has been recycled. This means that a vast part of the total plastic produced over the course of these 65 years has turned to waste (United Nations Environment Programme, 2021: 15–17). Plastic pollution has manifold implications for human individuals and communities. Plastic may contaminate soil and require yearly clean-ups, generating costs for farmers. Beaches littered with plastic may have a reduced attractiveness to tourists, leading to a decline of incoming visitors and subsequently a loss of income in the area. Plastic pollution also affects humans through their diet; microplastics have been found in 8 per cent of freshwater and 10 per cent of marine fish, including in fish destined for human consumption (United Nations Environment Programme, 2021: 40–44).

When considering the different facets of the environmental crisis, it is vital to understand that these developments are not isolated occurrences; they are interrelated and can be mutually reinforcing. Climate change, for example, leads to global warming and increases the likelihood of extreme weather events, which affect ecological systems and biodiversity negatively. Even with global warming in the range of 1.5°C to 2°C, 'the majority of terrestrial species ranges are projected to shrink dramatically. Changes in ranges can adversely affect the capacity of terrestrial protected areas to conserve species, greatly increase local species turnover and substantially increase the risk of global extinctions' (Díaz et al, 2019: 16). Within an interdependent system, the extinction of species has further implications. Among others, the loss of biodiversity decreases the resilience of ecological (and agrarian) systems to withstand the increased challenges caused by climate change. In a spiralling development, this contributes further to the extinction of species and the loss of biodiversity.

Situated within – and at the root of – the developments and trends that taken together can be labelled as an environmental crisis, is human activity. The influence that human activity has on shaping our world has grown over time. In contrast to earlier periods, when humanity's impact was limited, today human activity is at the root of major changes in earth systems. Against this background, it was suggested that 'we have entered a new planetary epoch, one in which human activities have become significant drivers of all major earth systems' (Bowden, 2017: 53), the **Anthropocene**. The basic argument underlying the idea of the Anthropocene is that a transition has taken place from a time when human activity was a marginal influence on the planet and earth systems to an era in which human activity is a major influence and driving force for development. While the Anthropocene draws considerably on geological and earth sciences to highlight the importance of human activity as a major driver impacting all earth systems, the concept of the Anthropocene is not only a scientific label; it is also used as a call for change (Bowden, 2017: 52–53).

As the concept of the Anthropocene gains increasing traction, debates remain over when this earth age began. In this context, major stepping stones in the continuously growing human impact have been identified. Humans shaped the earth for a long time, for instance through modification of habitat. Against this background, an early Anthropocene may have started about 2,000 years ago or even earlier. A major increase of human activity resulted from the **Industrial Revolution** around the turn of the 19th century. The Industrial Revolution marks an important change in human development. It contributed to growing urbanisation, and coincided with the start of more rapid population growth and technological and economic changes, which implied a shift from muscular power and wood as sources of energy to an increasing use of fossil fuels, a key driver, for instance, of climate change (see Chapter 10). A further important step that increased human impact was the **Great Acceleration**, which started in the middle of the 20th century. This period stands for a very sharp increase in the impact that human activity has had on the environment. Population growth, global economic growth and trade accelerated, agriculture intensified and so did humanity's environmental impact. To visualise the sharp increase, take the example of emissions. The main part of the rise of carbon dioxide emission since pre-industrial times occurred since the end of the Second World War (Zalasiewicz et al, 2015).

The environmental crisis and inequality

The environmental crisis has important implications for human individuals and societies. It affects humans at different levels, directly and individually, through disruptions of ecological systems, and via political and social changes, which stem from environmental changes.

Extreme heat, one of the consequences of climate change, for example, has important direct and individual consequences, particularly if it persists over a longer time. It has been linked to a range of health conditions, including, but not limited to, heat strokes and respiratory problems. Likewise, air pollution is linked to respiratory and cardiovascular diseases and an increased risk of lung cancer. Apart from obvious threats to lives, physical health, livelihood and property, disasters such as flooding have a negative impact on mental health (Stanke et al, 2012). The environmental crisis can also cause disruptions of ecological systems, which can affect humans. It can furthermore lead to social, economic and political changes. Take the example of rising sea levels, which threaten the very existence of small low-lying island states such as Kiribati or Tuvalu. If these islands were to disappear, inhabitants would lose their homes, properties and would probably have to migrate. In addition to leading to increased migration, which impacts the regions of reception, this would also have implications for the communities of these islands, who may find themselves scattered across different countries. This may, in turn, affect their cultural identity and sense of community and belonging.

The impact the environmental crisis has on individuals, communities and countries differs according to exposure, susceptibility and ability to cope. **Exposure** refers to 'the presence of people and their livelihoods, environmental resources and infrastructure, or economic, social or cultural assets in places that could be adversely affected by climate hazards' (United Nations Department of Economic and Social Affairs, 2020: 87). **Susceptibility** relates to the actual impact that an event may cause. To visualise this, imagine two individuals or communities, which experience the same weather event (for instance a flood). The damage to their properties may differ significantly depending, for instance, on the construction of their homes. This means they have different levels of susceptibility to the impacts of flooding. The **ability to cope** hinges on the resources that are available. At a personal level this includes (but is not limited to) material resources (for example, savings) and social networks. For countries, the level of income and the structure of the economy are key features that shape the ability to adapt to changing circumstances and to mitigate their impacts (United Nations Department of Economic and Social Affairs, 2020: 88).

Exposure, susceptibility and the ability to cope differ within countries. This means that the effects of the environmental crisis are not felt equally. The environmental crisis may have negative economic implications, particularly for poor households. People living in poverty are, for instance, more susceptible to the effects of climate change than are wealthier people in the same region (United Nations Department of Economic and Social Affairs, 2020: 8). To visualise this, take the example of food prices. Climate change may exacerbate price volatility. As poorer households have fewer economic resources on which they can draw to pay higher prices, food price increases impact poor consumers more than wealthy ones (International Food Policy Research Institute, 2011). Further, due to differing conditions and lived experiences (see Chapter 8), climate change is likely to have different implications according to, for instance, gender or age.

As exposure, susceptibility and the (especially financial and economic) ability to cope differ not only at an individual but also at a regional and national level, the effects of the environmental crisis are also not felt equally between countries. Climate change, for instance, is expected to increase mortality resulting from diarrhoea, malaria and dengue fever and may lead to more deaths caused by coastal flooding (World Health Organization, 2014). Given regional disparities in the prevalence of these events and diseases and the ability to mitigate them, it has been estimated that mortality rates in sub-Saharan Africa will be particularly affected by climate change, and Southeast Asia is expected to be especially affected by health impacts of climate change (United Nations Department of Economic and Social Affairs, 2020: 103). Further, climate change may result in higher food prices and lower food security, impacting access to drinking water and food, particularly for poor people in the Global South (Islam and Winkel, 2017).

Not only the impact but also the contribution to the environmental crisis is unequal. The negative environmental impact of humanity is caused disproportionately by a small subset of the world's population. Overall, the wealthier have a more pronounced negative environmental impact than their poorer counterparts. Take the example of the carbon footprint of households. In the European Union, those 10 per cent of the population who have the highest carbon footprint produce more carbon than the 50 per cent of the population who have the lowest carbon footprint. Those households with the highest carbon footprint tend to be those with the highest incomes and spending (Ivanova and Wood, 2020: 10). Taken together, this means that 'the groups likely to be affected the most are the ones least responsible for causing it' (Koch, 2021: 5).

Public services and the environmental crisis: between adaptation and mitigation

The environmental crisis also has important implications for public services. Take the example of climate change. It contributes to more frequent and intense extreme weather events, including flooding. If flooding increases, this raises the demands for emergency services, who oversee the situation, evacuate residents, care for the wounded, ensure public safety, and so on. Emergency services and public services who are not in the frontline of the response, like social services, need to adapt to the changing circumstances when delivering their services. **Adaptation** means that they need to adjust their way of working to account for occurring or predicted changes and their impacts, some of which have been outlined in this chapter. This 'involves changes that facilitate adjustment to actual or expected future climate, by moderating the harmful effects or taking advantage of beneficial opportunities arising from it' (United Nations Department of Economic and Social Affairs, 2020: 89). One key tool that helps prepare for these changes is the adaptation cycle, which is used in different contexts. Starting with the assessment of risks and vulnerabilities, the adaptation cycle encompasses the development of approaches, the analysis of (likely) impacts that these different approaches generate, and the decision for one approach as well as its implementation and evaluation. Monitoring, evaluation and review are essential components. Challenges result from the fact that environmental changes happen over long time periods, making it hard to assess the impact of specific actions. Uncertainties are furthermore caused by the fact that most of the effects of the environmental crisis will happen in the future, so that their exact extent and shape are unknown, which means that actions are based on expectations and predictions (European Environmental Agency, 2015: 18–21).

The relationship between public services and the environmental crisis is not limited to public services' need to adapt. Public services themselves have an environmental impact. The environmental impact that they generate can contribute to the environmental crisis. Reducing public services' environmental impact can be a part of broader changes to mitigate the environmental crisis. **Mitigation** in this context refers to slowing down the developments that taken together make the environmental crisis (for example, climate change or loss of biodiversity) (United Nations Department of Economic and Social Affairs, 2020: 89; how public services can contribute to mitigating climate change will be further explored in Chapter 10).

When considering how public services affect the environment, it is important to remember that the umbrella term *public services* encompasses a broad range of organisations (see Introduction). In some cases, the remit of these services and those working within them directly links to environmental considerations. State forest enterprises, for example, are public enterprises which are engaged in forest maintenance, regeneration and protection. Foresters monitor and sustain or improve the health of forests and woodlands. Countryside rangers monitor, maintain and develop the land and take proactive actions to sustain and improve areas. Sustainability Officers work alongside residents, communities and different organisations to promote more environmentally friendly practices. By their very nature, these public services and public servants aim to sustain wildlife and landscape and/or lessen humanity's environmental impact. Yet, even though a service may have a stated environmental focus, effective implementation and a positive environmental impact cannot be taken for granted. Therefore, it is essential to assess its real-life environmental impact (see Chapter 1). While for some public services environmental concerns are at the very heart of their nature and explicitly part of their remit, for others, environmental considerations, which have for a long time been absent or an afterthought, are gaining importance. Education services, for instance, increasingly aim to foster environmental knowledge and a better understanding of the environmental crisis and humanity's role therein. Increased knowledge and awareness fostered in educational settings may contribute to changing attitudes and behaviour in the future and pave the way for a broader shift towards more environmentally friendly practices. Thereby, these services can make a (albeit indirect) positive contribution to change and act as one important part of a broader strategy to decrease humanity's negative impact. Yet the impact of a service does not hinge on its remit alone.

While the aims and activities of specific public services may (or may not) include environmental considerations that contribute to strengthening attempts to reduce humanity's negative impact on the environment, all public services, including those with environmental aims and activities, also have an **ecological footprint**, which is generated through their workings, needs and actions. To establish the real-life impact, the environmental footprint that a particular public service has, it is essential to assess the impact generated by its operations. Public services, be they emergency services, social, health or education services, use spaces, which need to be heated. They use items that depend on energy use (for example, computers used to store and manage data). Some public services, like ambulance services or fire services, furthermore depend on the use of vehicles to fulfil their tasks. These preconditions in the form of heating, energy or transportation have an environmental impact (see Chapter 10).

Further, to function effectively, public services depend on a range of tools, from commonly used ones like computers, paper or office equipment like chairs or desks to specific tools such as medical equipment required by ambulance services. The production of these items has an environmental impact. It oftentimes involves the use of raw materials like earth metals used in IT hardware. The extraction of these raw materials is an intervention in ecological systems which has an impact on the environment. Likewise, the production process, which may involve energy use and the use of materials, affects the environment. In addition, production processes tend to create wastage, which affects the environment. Assessing the overall impact of each tool used by public services therefore means assessing not only their usage (including, for instance, the use of energy and cleaning requirements) but also the impact of the production process and how a tool affects the environment once it is discarded. The overall environmental impact of any given public service then derives from, first, the impact of their tasks in combination with, second, the impact generated by their work and, third, their consumption.

Trends and developments

In the light of increasing concerns about sustainability (see Chapter 7) and the environment more specifically, public services are increasingly required and/or urged to move towards more sustainable practices (see Chapter 10). To mitigate the environmental crisis, far-reaching changes are needed, from changing consumption choices and behaviour of individuals and mega consumers to re-envisioning production processes and infrastructure design.

Public services cannot mitigate the environmental crisis on their own. Yet they can play an important part in broader strategies. Thereby, it is not only the actions of individual services that are important; the way in which public services interact with each other and other organisations also shapes the environmental impact. Some key trends in trying to contribute to mitigate the environmental crisis, at a general level as well as regarding public services more specifically, are outlined in the following.

A first important development is a trend towards a (more) **circular economy**. The interrelatedness of economic processes and the environment is the starting point for the idea of a circular economy. To fully capture the idea of the circular economy, it is vital to recognise that the economy and the environment are intrinsically linked and interconnected; the economy is based on using natural resources as input for production and consumption and as a *vessel* for waste (see the considerations on the creation of waste in the subsection 'Public services and the environmental crisis: between adaptation and mitigation'). At the same time, our natural environment, the earth, is a closed and circular system. Drawing on these basic insights, ideas around the circular economy are based on the premise that to safeguard the viability and sustainability of our natural environment, the economy and the environment need to be kept in balance. Consequently, the circular economy envisions an economic system that respects the environment and is based on a balanced coexistence of both the economy and the environment. Promoting a circular economy means, for example, fostering recycling and reusing materials, or – in other words – creating an economy where 'material flows keep circulating … without entering the biosphere unless they are biological nutrients' (Kalmykova et al, 2018). The ideas of the circular economy have increasingly reached public sector organisations, who, in turn, progressively include circular economy considerations in their operations by revisiting the tools they use and purchase and by fostering recycling, remanufacturing and refurbishment rather than purchasing new items. Changes that public sector organisations have made to support a more circular economy range from small-scale change (such as distributing reusable mugs to employees) to reusing equipment, recycling uniforms and adopting circular approaches to heating and the use of water (Klein et al, 2021), and changing public procurement practices (see Box 9.1).

Box 9.1: Greening school catering

Seeking to improve its environmental impact, the city of Turin in Italy turned its attention to catering in schools, which is a contracted service. With about eight million school meals delivered each year and a total cost to the city of about €40 million, catering in schools is an important activity and Turin aimed to use its position as an important consumer to promote more environmentally friendly practices. When assessing the impact of catering, it is vital to understand that a range of activities associated with school catering create the overall environmental impact, from the preparation of the food to its transportation and the plates it is served on. Turin's approach to reduce the environmental impact of its school catering encompassed a range of different aspects, including but not limited to buying more energy-efficient appliances and reducing the environmental impact of transport. In line with the ideas of the circular economy, particular attention was given to reducing waste by promoting reusable and biodegradable products. To this aim, Turin encouraged those delivering the services to use reusable and refillable products and biodegradable packaging. To improve the environmental impact of associated activities, such as cleaning, Turin also promoted the use of ecological cleaning products (European Commission, 2014).

Indigenous knowledge can be an important source of insight and inspiration for re-envisioning the things public services do in a more environmentally friendly manner. Generally, Indigenous cultures, from the Sámi in Finland, Norway, Russia and Sweden to Canada's First Nations, tend to have a more intertwined vision of humanity and the environment (see Chapter 7), which conceives humanity and its environment as inherently interrelated and interdependent and features stronger considerations of balancing humanity's environmental impact. Learning from Indigenous knowledge includes revitalising and promoting Indigenous practices in their area of origin as well as learning from Indigenous practices in other parts of the world. One example of the positive environmental impact that drawing on Indigenous and traditional knowledge and traditions can have is the transformation of public buildings into green spaces, which can improve water management, help prevent floods and be used to grow crops (see Box 9.2).

Box 9.2: Bangkok's Thammasat University

Indigenous building practices are increasingly becoming an inspiration for architects, who seek to build (more) sustainably. One example of this trend is the Thammasat University in Bangkok. Taking inspiration from traditional Thai rice terraces, the Thammasat University building features an h-shaped roof, whose sides descend in zigzagging vertically arranged spaces, which serve as a space to grow and produce food. Over 40 edible kinds of crops are grown on the roof of the building, creating a source of food production in a city that experiences scarcity. However, the benefits of the building's design are more than creating a green space and room for planting foods. By returning to traditional building practices, this building uses traditional knowledge of water management. In combination with the shape of the building, this planted green roof slows down the flow of rainwater, an important feature in a city that increasingly experiences periodic floods. Further, the building and the planted soil collects, stores and filters water (Wang, 2020).

To identify and subsequently adopt more environmentally friendly behaviours and actions, **awareness** of environmental challenges and developments, and knowledge of structural connections and the contribution of individual actions to broader developments are indispensable. Public services and education services as dispensers of knowledge, in particular, can play an important role by promoting awareness and knowledge of environmental issues. By creating awareness and promoting environmental knowledge among the wider population, public services can promote environmentally friendly practices at a broader societal level. In this vein, the United Nations Educational, Scientific and Cultural Organization (UNESCO) highlights that 'education must change to create a peaceful and sustainable world for the survival and prosperity of current and future generations' (UNESCO, 2020: iii). Given the impact that education can have, different initiatives seek to integrate environmental and sustainability knowledge into education. To support this transformation, UNESCO (2020) developed and published a roadmap for *Education for Sustainable Development*, which outlines key fields of activity and provides guidance for its implementation.

Summary

One of the core challenges in today's world is the environmental crisis, which encompasses different yet intersecting and interacting facets, from climate change and pollution to the extinction of species and the loss of biodiversity. At the root of this environmental crisis is human activity, including activities linked to the delivery of public services. Over the past centuries, the importance of human activity for the development of the earth systems has grown significantly, leading to a new era in which human activity is a major driver for development – the Anthropocene.

The environmental crisis has important implications for public services. It affects the conditions under which public services operate and requires public services to adapt to this changing environment. At the same time as being affected by the environmental crisis, public services contribute to shaping the development of the earth systems. By virtue of their core functions, specific public services, which focus on or include environmental aims, may have a positive impact on the environment. This is particularly the case for services that aim to maintain or improve the environment. In addition, components of daily activities in public services affect the environment, be it emissions generated by ambulances or fire engines, or energy used to heat office spaces. Also, activities that relate to (and are necessary for) the delivery of public services, such as cleaning ambulances or offices, contribute to the environmental impact of public services. Public services also generate an impact through their consumption. To fulfil their tasks, public services depend on a range of different tools. The production of these uses (natural) resources and creates wastage. At the end of their lifecycle, these goods and tools often are discarded, which adds further to public services' environmental impact. The overall environmental impact of a particular service results from the specific combination of the impact of its task, its daily activities and its consumption. The impact generated by a service's activities is thereby also the starting point for public services' engagement in mitigating the environmental crisis.

While far-reaching changes which exceed the scope of public services' activities are needed to mitigate the environmental crisis, public services can play an important part in broader shifts to limit environmental damage. They can limit their environmental impact by considering their consumption choices and be part of a move towards a (more) circular economy. Further, public services can act as promoters of knowledge. Education services in particular can play an essential role in creating awareness and promoting environmental knowledge.

Key points

- From increasing pollution to the extinction of species and the loss of biodiversity and climate change, the earth is facing an unprecedented crisis. At the root of this crisis is human activity.
- The environmental crisis affects public services, who must adapt to new challenges.
- Public services have an environmental impact, which is shaped by the work they carry out, the emissions and wastage produced, and the environmental impact of resources and tools required for the functioning of the service.
- Public services can play an important part in broader strategies to mitigate the environmental crisis. They can limit their negative environmental impact, for example by revisiting their consumption choices, promoting a circular economy, and fostering environmental knowledge and awareness.

Questions

- Which features determine the impact of the environmental crisis on individuals and communities?
- What is characterised by the term Anthropocene?
- In what ways are public services impacted by the environmental crisis?
- In what ways are public services implicated in the environmental crisis?
- What can public services do to become active stakeholders in the effort to mitigate the environmental crisis?

Further reading

Robbins, P., Hintz, J. and Moore, S.A. (2014) *Environment and society: A critical introduction*, Hoboken: Wiley-Blackwell. *This book examines theoretical approaches and conceptual tools for understanding environmental issues.*

Schlottmann, C., Jerolmack, C., Rademacher, A., Damon, M. and Jamieson, D. (eds) (2017) *Environment and society: A reader*, New York: New York University Press. *This book brings together core readings on the environment and its relationship to society.*

References

Bowden, G. (2017) 'An environmental sociology for the Anthropocene', *Canadian Review of Sociology*, 54(1): 48–68.

Díaz, S., Settele, J., Brondízio, E.S., Ngo, H.T., Guèze, M., Agard, J., Arneth, A., Balvanera, P., Brauman, K.A., Butchart, S.H.M., Chan, K.M.A., Garibaldi, L.A., Ichii, K., Liu, J., Subramanian, S.M., Midgley, G.F., Miloslavich, P., Molnár, Z., Obura, D., Pfaff, A., Polasky, S., Purvis, A., Razzaque, J., Reyers, B., Roy, R., Chowdhury, R., Shin, Y.J., Visseren-Hamakers, I.J., Willis, K.J. and Zayas, C.N. (eds) (2019) *Summary for policymakers of the global assessment report on biodiversity and ecosystem services of the Intergovernmental Science-Policy Platform on Biodiversity and Ecosystem Services*, Bonn: IPBES secretariat, available at: https://doi.org/10.5281/zenodo.3553579 [Accessed 24 January 2022].

European Commission (2014) *Monitoring low carbon, sustainable catering services: City of Turin, Italy. GPP in practice, no 47*, available at: https://ec.europa.eu/environment/gpp/pdf/news_alert/Issue47_Case_Study100_Turin.pdf [Accessed 24 January 2022].

European Environmental Agency (2015) *National monitoring, reporting and evaluation of climate change adaptation in Europe: Technical report no 20/2015*, available at: https://www.eea.europa.eu/publications/national-monitoring-reporting-and-evaluation [Accessed 24 January 2022].

International Food Policy Research Institute (2011) *2011 global food policy report*, available at: https://reliefweb.int/sites/reliefweb.int/files/resources/oc72.pdf [Accessed 24 January 2022].

Islam, N.S. and Winkel, J. (2017) *Climate change and social inequality*, Department of Economic & Social Affairs, DESA Working Paper No 152, available at: https://www.un.org/esa/desa/papers/2017/wp152_2017.pdf [Accessed 24 January 2022].

Ivanova, D. and Wood, R. (2020) 'The unequal distribution of household carbon footprints in Europe and its link to sustainability', *Global Sustainability*, 3(e18): 1–12, available at: https://doi.org/10.1017/sus.2020.12 [Accessed 24 January 2022].

Kalmykova, Y., Sadagopan, M. and Rosado, L. (2018) 'Circular economy: From review of theories and practices to development of implementation tools', *Resources, Conservation & Recycling*, 135(2018): 190–201.

Klein, N., Ramos, T.B. and Deutz, P. (2021) 'Advancing the circular economy in public sector organisations: Employees' perspectives on practices', *Circular Economy and Sustainability*, available at: https://doi.org/10.1007/s43615-021-00044-x [Accessed 24 January 2022].

Koch, M. (2021) 'Social policy without growth: Moving towards sustainable welfare states', *Social Policy and Society*, 1–13, available at: doi:10.1017/S1474746421000361 [Accessed 24 January 2022].

Stanke, C., Murray, V., Amlôt, R., Nurse, J.O. and Williams, R. (2012) 'The effects of flooding on mental health: Outcomes and recommendations from a review of the literature', *PLoS Currents*, 4, available at: doi: 10.1371/4f9f1fa9c3cae [Accessed 24 January 2022].

United Nations Department of Economic and Social Affairs (2020) *World social report 2020: Inequality in a rapidly changing world*, available at: https://www.un.org/development/desa/dspd/wp-content/uploads/sites/22/2020/01/World-Social-Report-2020-FullReport.pdf [Accessed 24 January 2022].

United Nations Educational, Scientific and Cultural Organisation (2020) *Education for sustainable development: A roadmap*, Paris: United Nations Educational, Scientific and Cultural Organisation.

United Nations Environment Programme (2021) *Neglected: Environmental justice impacts of marine litter and plastic pollution*, Nairobi: United Nations Environment Programme.

Wang, L. (2020) 'Asia's largest organic rooftop farm can grow 20 tons of food annually', *INHABITAT*, 15 September, available at: https://inhabitat.com/asias-largest-organic-rooftop-farm-can-grow-20-tons-of-food-annually/ [Accessed 28 January 2022].

World Health Organization (2014) *Quantitative risk assessment of the effects of climate change on selected causes of death, 2030s and 2050s*, Geneva: World Health Organization.

Zalasiewicz, J., Waters, W.M., Barnosky, A.D., Cearreta, A., Crutzen, P., Ellis, E., Ellis, M.A., Fairchild, I.J., Grinevald, J., Haff, P.K., Hajdas, I., Leinfelder, R., McNeill, J., Odada, E.O., Poirier, C., Richter, D., Steffen, W., Summerhayes, C., Syvitski, J.P.M., Vidas, D., Wagreich, M., Wing, S.L., Wolfe, A.P., Zhisheng, A. and Oreskes, N. (2015) 'When did the Anthropocene begin? A mid-twentieth century boundary level is stratigraphically optimal', *Quaternary International*, 383: 196–203.

10

Adapting organisations: public services, climate change and the energy transition

Filippos Proedrou

Chapter objectives

Focusing on climate change, this chapter outlines how the topic has gained increasing importance on the political agenda and explores the role of public service organisations as actors. Climate change and the progressing energy transition calls for all actors, including public services, to change the way they operate and work around their goals. In this evolving context and disruptive reality, public services are active actors of change. This chapter demonstrates how public services use their multiple competences and policy tools, agenda-/goals-setting, policy formulation and policy implementation. It secondly explores further avenues of upscaling climate action, such as increasing climate and energy ambition, intensification of the conversion of operations away from fossil fuels and towards clean energy, and different employment structures. Third, this chapter showcases how taking this direction chimes with increasing demand and a more favourable political, economic and social environment for a climate-sensitive modus operandi of public services.

Introduction

Public services perform essential duties and thus lie at the core of central provisions for human welfare, such as healthcare, emergency responses and so on (see Introduction). Thereby, public services are active agents, actors in shaping policymaking and implementation (see Chapter 1). To adapt to a changing environment, public services need to adjust and manage change (see Chapters 4 and 5). Particularly in the face of essential challenges, such as the environmental crisis (see Chapter 9), they need, however, to go beyond small-scale steps and become active actors in mitigation. This chapter brings together the insights from the previous chapters to explore public services as actors and adapting organisations within a changing world. Therefore, it takes one of the core challenges of our time, climate change, as a focus point.

The starting point for this chapter is the fact that public services generate an extensive carbon and ecological footprint, which leads to them becoming part of the climate change challenge (see Chapter 9). Defined as the identifiable large-scale shifts in the state of the planet's climate over long periods, climate change forces humanity to reshuffle the way it produces, trades and consumes energy, because more than four-fifths of greenhouse gas emissions are caused by the combustion of fossil fuels. This brings forward the need for the overhaul of the energy systems (commonly referred to as energy transition), which expands to all sectors (for example, transportation, power generation, buildings, land use), concerns all actors (public services, governmental, corporate, individuals and so on), and has repercussions for our everyday mode of living. With differentiated impacts of climate change, this need to mitigate climate change, furthermore, has important implications for the state of equality within and between countries (see Chapters 8 and 9).

Climate change hence calls on all public and private actors to delve into and contribute to the design and implementation of a profound and extensive energy transition. The shortcut of the global energy transition is the substitution of fossil fuel production, trade and consumption with the generation of clean energy, such as solar and wind energy, and the establishment of clean energy systems. In this understanding, public services need to adjust to a new reality of a changing global climate and turn from part of the problem to a pillar for the solution, while not sacrificing efficiency in the delivery of services. What is essentially called for from public services actors is to disentangle from the fossil-based structures of the economy while they embark on restructuring the provision of public services through clean modes of energy production, trade and consumption.

The chapter proceeds as follows. The next section provides an account of the state of scientific knowledge on climate change, expanding on discussions in the previous chapter. In doing so, it sets out the broader policy context and the principal trends in the beginning of the third decade of the 21st century. The first subsection focuses on how global and local political developments, more ambitious climate brinkmanship, changing market fundamentals and augmenting societal pressure increasingly place climate change on the political agenda (see Chapter 1) and create a more conducive environment for public services actors to double down on their climate and energy transition-compatible agendas. The second subsection then provides a categorisation of the main public services actors, and the policy tools at their disposal. This subsection singles out their goals/agenda setting, policy formulation and policy implementation (see Chapter 1) competences. The following section delves into the agendas and measures public services actors have taken up to adjust to climate change and tackle energy transition challenges, and provides case studies to illustrate the more general points made, such as how strategic investments and management decisions impact public services' carbon footprint. The fourth section scrutinises the main remaining gaps in terms of ambition setting and cascading action that would further bolster public services' climate agendas and energy transitions. The fifth section sums up the main points of this chapter. This chapter then brings together ideas about policymaking (see Chapter 1), the creation of effective strategies (see Chapter 5) and sustainability techniques (see Chapter 7) to provide innovative tools to address issues raised in this and the previous chapter.

Setting the policy context for public service actors in the climate change era

Climate change as a challenge

Humanity has reached critical planetary boundaries across most natural resource indices, such as rate of biodiversity loss, global freshwater use and ocean acidification (see Chapter 9). The quest for sustainability, understood as a three-dimensional model that includes the maintenance of sufficient natural capital (the environment) so that it can be reproduced indefinitely and support human wellbeing (the social) and the generation of economic wealth in the future (the economy) (Daly, 1996), has entered policymaking discourses (see Chapter 7). A core element of sustainable development is effective climate change mitigation to stabilise the global temperature increase ideally to 1.5°C, and to no more than 2°C. Due to fossil energy's (coal, oil and gas) central role in the release of greenhouse gases that cause climate change, the overhaul of the modes of energy production, trade and consumption becomes a pivotal issue in the global climate change mitigation enterprise.

In this changing context, public services need to maintain, and improve, their provision, while restructuring their modus operandi in line with climate imperatives and energy transitions benchmarks. On the one hand, there are many synergies between public services' environmental, economic and social goals that can be exploited. Ambitious climate goals include promoting active transport (walking, cycling) and radically reducing transport by means of petrol and diesel fuelled cars. Besides reducing emissions, this would improve people's health and, in doing so, alleviate pressure from the overburdened national health systems. To provide another example, mandating regular energy auditing of public and private infrastructure and premises, and financing sustainable energy solutions, helps bring down long-term costs, while generating new employment positions and averting path dependence on expensive fossil energy systems. What is at stake is for public services actors to design and implement policies (see Chapter 1) that generate positive outcomes across the environmental–social–economic nexus which characterises sustainability (see Chapter 7). In short, public services must adapt to and contribute to mitigating climate change; thereby, innovation is a crucial tool.

As has already been argued in Chapter 7, *policy goals and the three dimensions of sustainability are often conflicting*. Environmental, economic and social interests and benefits do not always converge, and hence public services actors face dilemmas or trilemmas in their decision-making process. Regarding climate change, the most clear-cut conflict is the competition for resources between projects that aim to increase clean energy availability and access on the one hand, and projects that will serve social policy agendas, such as poverty alleviation, on the other. This competition only becomes starker in times of austerity, when state budgets shrink further, thus rendering the need for further cuts and goal/project prioritisation more acute (see Chapter 7).

At a second, more profound level, there is a tension between public services' ambition to expand their remit and services on the one hand, and the imperative to operate within physical constraints, as mandated by climate change, on the other. In other words, public services need to balance the need to expand their services and to do so within limited physical boundaries. These trade-offs can perhaps be better understood in terms of different timeframes (see Chapter 5). While in the long-term policies that advance the energy transition will also reap economic and social benefits, in the short-term funnelling substantial amounts of investments and policy entrepreneurship to the energy transition may compromise sound finance and other pressing social goals (such as combating homelessness or promoting equality) (Van de Graaf and Sovacool, 2020). Overall, the challenge for public services in the climate change era is how to design and implement innovative policies so that social and economic agendas do not come at the cost of the energy transition.

Non-energy transition compatible strategies are no longer an option

With sustainability as an emerging trend across sectors and contexts (see Chapter 7), however, the days when the trilemma for policymakers, as well as for those implementing policies, such as public services actors, among environmental, economic and social benefits was by default resolved to the detriment of the former are gone for good. While environmental aspects of policymaking have for a long time been considered a luxury when public services actors were faced with pressing social and economic priorities, now environmental concerns are increasingly couched in economic and social terms. This change stems from different developments. First, climate change has reached a point where action is indispensable, rather than an option to be debated. Second, as the famous Stern report (2006) has shown, delaying climate action and the energy transition amounts to higher economic costs and burdens for the following years' budgets. Climate action and the energy transition are also increasingly analysed through the prism of higher economic and social gains, such as employment opportunities, better health and higher welfare levels.

Two other factors increasingly tilt the balance in favour of environmental preoccupations. The first is the changing timeframe for climate action. Since the Intergovernmental Panel on Climate Change's (IPCC) 2019 report highlighted the need to reconsider the world's climate ambition closer towards the 1.5°C goal for 2050, and to substantially increase the climate goals for 2030, embedding climate goals in policymaking at all levels has become a necessity. This has also both corroborated and empowered the second factor, the increasing societal pressure to eventually take the climate crisis seriously, placing the topic firmly on the political agenda (see Chapter 1).

Moreover, the operationalisation of climate change goals is taking shape. Since the signing of the Paris Agreement in 2015, where most of the world's states agreed to make transparent climate commitments at a unilateral level, submit climate action plans, and review their commitments and action plans every five years, the long-needed global operational and accountability framework has been put in place. A well-based optimism reigns in that the peer review mechanism and the diffusion of best practices globally will encourage and facilitate states to increase their level of ambition and commitment of resources to their climate change mitigation agendas (Falkner, 2016). In general, more transparent, concrete and ambitious climate goals set by governments will inevitably trickle down towards public services actors, who will need to upscale their energy and action plans.

In this changing context, where climate change is increasingly an important part of the political agenda, public services actors can choose among many decarbonisation avenues to mitigate climate change, but they are deprived of the choice to continue business as usual. Changing market fundamentals facilitate a gradual switch in mindsets. Clean energy costs have come down exponentially. In many cases, there is a clear-cut business case in favour of clean energy sources, especially solar and wind, vis-à-vis fossil fuels, even when the necessary upfront costs are taken into account. Possibilities in the energy efficiency, heating and electro-mobility sectors also multiply and proliferate, again making it easier for public services actors to explore different decarbonisation pathways at the same time. This allows public services to draw on and promote innovation in tackling the crisis and bring about strategic change (see Chapters 4 and 5).

Public services' importance as actors for the mitigation of climate change

The global energy transition cannot be implemented by means of single large initiatives and policies emanating from the global level. As Ostrom (2009) has persuasively shown, effective climate action, including a fast-track energy transition, calls for a polycentric strategy (see Chapter 5); that is, an approach composed of different centres, that involves cooperation between public and private actors (see Chapter 2) at local, national, regional and global levels (see Chapter 3). The significance of public services in this collective endeavour is hard to underestimate. Recent legislative developments that set targets (see Chapter 4), including most importantly the goal of carbon neutrality (defined as the state in which carbon emissions released can be absorbed by the global ecosystem) by 2050, place limitations on public services sectors' carbon budget, the total amount of carbon they can emit within a defined timeframe (IPCC, 2019). Beyond such legal requirements, public services are established institutions with significant competences, budgets and leverage that can significantly advance the energy transition agenda. More specifically, public services play crucial roles in different stages of the policy cycle (see Chapter 1). They can influence/set agendas and goals, formulate/influence policies through *regulation* and planning competences, and *implement policies* through strategic and daily decisions in terms of energy transition schemes and sustainable public procurement (see Chapters 1, 5 and 7).

More specifically, restructuring public services' operations in line with energy transition requirements involves three parallel processes. First, the termination of investments in fossil fuel-related industries (negative screening – terminating the purchase of diesel or petrol vehicles). Second, investment exclusively in clean energy sources and systems and in industries that embrace ecologically sustainable processes (positive screening – contracting 100 per cent of energy supply through clean energy). Third, withdrawal from any investments in fossil fuel-related industries and activities (fossil divestment – the divestment of public services' pension funds from fossil-linked assets) (Mocatta and White, 2020).

Under the umbrella term of public services, there are a multitude of different actors with varying competences, strengths and weaknesses (see Chapter 2), leverage, and ambition to support climate change and energy transition agendas. The remainder of this chapter focuses on the role of a variety of public service organisations, from across sectors (private, public and voluntary) and across government levels (local, national, supranational, global), as actors (see Chapter 1). These actors dispose of different soft and hard assets and competences to implement policies and improve their climate and energy credentials and performance. These assets can be broken down to: leeway to manage budgets (in terms of expenditure and staffing among others), demand creation through public procurement, network and peer influence, negotiating power with state authorities and the corporate sector, social capital, and the power of example through the diffusion of best practices.

What all these services share is ample leverage over **policy implementation** (see Chapter 1). More specifically, the way they handle their significant budgets – including, among others, strategic investment decisions as part of their strategic management (see Chapter 5) as well as daily public procurement choices (see Chapter 7) – has a huge impact on the modes of energy consumed and the level of emissions released. Civil services and local authorities also retain ample leverage in **policy formulation** (see Chapter 1) through their regulatory competences. On top of these competences, local authorities have the added power of setting the agenda, understood as a separate policymaking stage preceding and defining the basic parameters of policy formulation, by means of establishing climate goals and designing action plans. The other public services actors also have agenda-/goals-setting competences, but they are limited to their internal policies and goals in terms of emissions reductions. Table 10.1 highlights the range of policy tools that can be used by public services actors and Table 10.2 shows actions they can take.

Table 10.1: Key public services actors and their main policy tools

Key actors	Agenda-/goal-setting at local/internal level	Policy formulation: regulation and planning (including land use)	Policy implementation: use of budget, investments, public procurement and consumption practices
Local authorities	√	√	√
National, supranational and global civil service/ bureaucracies	√	√	√
Emergency response services	√		√
Utilities, media, hospitals and universities	√		√

Table 10.2: Key public services actors and indicative key actions

Key actors	Indicative key actions
Local authorities	Climate plans and emissions goals Buildings and energy efficiency standards Facilitation of energy investments Minimisation/rationalisation of energy usage Switch to electric vehicle fleet and zero-energy buildings Clean energy generation
National, supranational and global civil service/bureaucracies	Energy efficiency standards Minimisation/rationalisation of energy usage Guidance for goal-setting and best practices
Emergency response services	Switch to electric vehicle fleet and zero-energy buildings Minimisation/rationalisation of energy usage Clean energy generation
Utilities, media, hospitals and universities	Energy auditing and investment on appliances Switch to zero-energy buildings Minimisation/rationalisation of energy usage Clean energy generation

Public services as actors in the energy transition

Local authorities' competences and policy tools vary in different national contexts. Nevertheless, they all command significant leverage through their agenda- and goal-setting, **regulation**, and land-use planning competences, as well as the leverage to decide on the sizeable budgets they operate, particularly via strategic investments and daily consumption. First, local authorities can set their ambitions at specific levels, influencing the extent of demand for clean energy structures and systems and associated services. Setting ambitious targets circumscribes the carbon budget, both influencing and mandating the operation of all public services actors within these carbon limits. Second, and associated with the previous point, local authorities can set energy efficiency and consumption standards, thus mandating specific requirements that impact on levels of energy use and emissions release. For example, energy efficiency standards incorporated in building directives influence the level of energy consumption in the building sector. Local authorities are also in charge of land–use planning. Afforestation, permits/licences for land use for clean energy facilities, and decisions on the scale of new projects to be undertaken in publicly owned local territory, all belong to the remit of local authorities, impact modes of energy production and consumption, and influence levels of emissions released.

This also determines urban sprawl and modes of transportation that directly affect levels of emissions and energy consumption. More broadly, local authorities take strategic decisions, such as a congestion tax to discourage car use (as London has done), or a prohibition on petrol cars travelling within the city centre (as Bristol Council has legislated), or the construction of cycling routes to encourage active travel (as in Münster, Leuven). To provide further examples, Cardiff Council committed £6.6 million to help Cardiff Bus to procure Ultra Low Emission Buses in its 2021 budget. Local authorities also have the competence to switch to an electric vehicle fleet for all their services, as well as invest themselves in clean energy generation, remake their own buildings as zero–carbon or passive buildings, and more generally procure in a more sustainable way across the value chain (see Chapter 7). In Germany, local authorities' investments in renewable energy have effectively reshuffled modes of energy production, supply and consumption, with municipalities increasingly managing their energy supply on their own and to varying extents covering their energy needs through clean energy investments and production. It is estimated that these municipal utilities account for around half of the country's electricity, gas and heat supply, playing a central role in Germany's energy transition and improving climate performance (Wagner et al, 2021). The Greek islands present another interesting example (see Box 10.1).

Box 10.1: Greece's green islands

Local authorities on small islands in the Aegean in Greece have taken bold steps to overhaul their energy supply. Having invested in solar and wind energy, hydro and pump storage, and clean energy micro-grids, they have (to varying extents) ensured their self-sufficiency in energy supply. Clean energy initiatives have facilitated energy supply in the islands, which has previously been catered for by volatile sub-sea lines. The case of Tilos, a small island in the Dodecanese, stands out, as the island became the first fully autonomous green island in the Mediterranean in 2018. Other Greek islands have also turned to green solutions, with the local authorities in Kythnos and Ikaria most prominently utilising a different mix of clean energy supply. In 2019, the local authorities of several Greek (and other European) islands published their clean energy transition plans. Seizing on financial and institutional support from the European Commission, Sifnos, Samos and Crete are moving into clean energy supply to improve both their energy security and their climate performance and credentials.

At a higher political level, national civil service teams are central in the climate and energy transition agendas in two main ways. First, they are essential in influencing the decision-making process regarding *regulation* and legislation. Their role in the policy cycle is pivotal, as the civil service provides the expertise and know-how that informs policymaking. It also provides the memory, the organisational structure and the context within which central decisions are taken (for example, regarding the level of ambition in terms of emissions reduction, share of clean energy in the energy mix and energy efficiency). *Regulations* on the use of specific building and energy efficiency standards, and on certain industrial and certification processes in terms of sustainable modes of production, have an extensive impact on the carbon intensity of the economy and on the levels of emissions released. Second, civil services also command authority over large budgets. As is the case with local authorities, public procurement decisions (see Chapter 7) make an impact both in terms of energy consumption and by means of setting an example of what is feasible and potentially preferable from both an energy-environmental and a financial perspective.

Going a step further, supranational institutions have also risen to become significant actors in the climate change battle and the energy transition. These institutions can be understood as the corollary of global civil service teams and global/supranational bureaucracy. For example, at a global level, the United Nations Economic and Social Council and Secretariat lie at the centre of the United Nations' Sustainable Development Goals of 2015 (see Chapters 3 and 7), where climate change mitigation and energy transition loom large, providing incentives, guidelines and benchmarks for more ambitious climate action. The United Nations' IPCC has been central to the global climate change mitigation and energy transition effort. The IPCC highlights the changing nature of climate science, the dangers climate change carries for humanity, and forecasts and proposes measures for action.

In the UK, this crucial epistemic role of translating climate science into tangible economic plans lies in the hands of the independent Climate Change Committee (CCC). Its recommendations are so authoritative that it is hard for UK national governments to oppose them; effectively, the CCC sets the goals and pace of the energy transition. The UK's plans to finance the energy transition more generously, as well as upscaling the country's climate goals and performance, have come as a response to direr forecasts and more urgent calls for climate action by the CCC (see Box 10.2).

> **Box 10.2:** The UK Climate Change Committee
>
> Established in 2008 under the provisions of the Climate Change Act, the CCC plays a very influential role in the formulation of the UK's climate policy. More specifically, the CCC provides its specialised recommendations to the UK and the devolved governments of Wales, Scotland and Northern Ireland (see Chapter 3) regarding the level of the climate ambition, goals and plans. Its scientific expertise means that the carbon budgets of UK governments and local authorities follow the CCC guidelines. The CCC also monitors compliance with set goals and drafts reports on best practices and emerging technologies that could be utilised in the energy transition. The CCC is essentially the go-to place for advice on climate change and energy transition and, unlike most other civil service actors, due to its special advisory status also enjoys competence and ample leverage over agenda- and goal-setting.

The emergency response services are unique among all the organisations defined as public services (see Chapter 2). The way they spend their budget and their example-setting role stand out as the most important functions these actors can play. The police and fire services, as well as the military, are based on expansive premises, are operating sizeable budgets, and modernise their equipment, vehicles and so on at regular times. Operating in a sustainable way makes a great difference in terms of energy consumption and levels of emissions released (and can increase demand for clean energy products and services). Nevertheless, public services can also transform how they think about their relation to energy. Rather than just using cleaner energy, public services can, however, use the land they hold to generate energy themselves, converting the land and buildings required into a source of sustainable energy. The innovation of becoming clean energy generators rather than consumers would allow these actors to move beyond simply converting into sustainable actors, and to also generate surplus clean energy that could offset the energy consumption of other actors and thereby promote change at a wider level.

Since the liberalisation era of the 1980s and the rise of the **New Public Management** dogma (see Chapters 2 and 4), many public services have been privatised or contracted out (see Chapters 2 and 7). While across the world there is a variety of ownership models for these actors, utilities, media, hospitals and universities are central in providing key public services to citizens. To start with utilities, it is obvious that their role is critical for rates of energy consumption and subsequent levels of emissions reductions (see Box 10.3). Utilities increasingly invest in clean energy projects and procure clean energy. This trend has been supported through government schemes such as feed-in tariffs and renewables obligations certificates. Still, however, utilities by and large do not tap into the large potential that lies within the systematic auditing of the energy consumption of the households and the industrial clients they supply, and within the provision of advice on and investment in clients' appliances that can bring overall energy consumption levels down.

> **Box 10.3:** A changing role and business model for utilities: an example from Sacramento
>
> Utilities' core business model has traditionally been to source and supply energy to customers at a profit. Most utilities have retained this business model, with the only alteration being the gradual switch towards cleaner energy portfolios. An alternative approach could be to focus on energy auditing and subsequent investment in clients' energy appliances and performance (under the reasonable assumption that for many consumers appliance substitution is expensive and not profitable over the first years and will not be undertaken despite the obvious long-term financial, energy and climate benefits involved). One utility in Sacramento has successfully implemented such a policy decades ago, bringing overall energy costs and emissions down. This scheme is feasible, if not preferable, also from a financial perspective for two reasons. Consumers could see their bills go down as they would consume far fewer energy units, albeit at higher unit prices so that the investment costs can be recovered. Utilities would thus need to source overall lower amounts of energy thus exploring a niche for further profits (Jackson, 1996). Such an alternative approach to *delivery of services* will have a significant *impact on the service user*, both from a financial and a climate-related perspective.

Public services with a focus on welfare such as education and health share some distinct characteristics: in many countries they comprise services delivered by private actors and voluntary organisations that provide fundamental public goods for citizens' welfare, they command large budgets, and they enjoy high coverage and reputation for their work. First, a rationalisation and minimisation of energy consumption of these actors would see a significant impact on the reduction of emissions (see Chapter 9). This would begin with sustainable procurement across the value chain (see Chapter 7), would include clear targets and monitoring as well as energy audits to provide accountability (see Chapter 4), and could reveal the areas with and extent of the potential for energy performance improvements to build the base for strategic management and investment decisions (see Chapter 5). Second, these actors dispose of significant assets, including land and finance, which could be used for the generation of clean energy. The University of Queensland, in Australia, for example, has established and operates a multimillion-dollar solar farm to offset its annual electricity needs. Beyond the tangible energy cuts benefits, such moves would constitute best practices that could be diffused to and reproduced across society and the business world. Third, these actors also hold significant shares in the fossil-fuel industry. Divestment from fossil fuels is a necessary step for public services actors so that they do not implicitly contradict their climate agendas. The University of California, Berkeley, for example, is one of the few that announced in 2019 that it would fully divest from its (around US$200 billion) fossil investment portfolio.

Trends and developments

Going a step further, it is critical to think about how public services actors can facilitate the transition by means of small, forward-looking innovations. Their organisational structures and charts have not been devised, and are hence not suitable, for the current and future changes (see Chapter 4), including but not limited to energy transition. In most cases, there is shortage of staff, of time in existing staff's workload and of required know-how, which are essential for successful implementation (see Chapters 1 and 7). For example, universities, hospitals and schools would benefit from creating one or more dedicated positions for energy officers (see Chapter 7).

What seems to be lacking, however, from the perspective of public services in most cases is an astute understanding that the climate crisis forces upon them the need to take a leading role in the energy transition. Even the most forward-looking public services focus on improving their energy and climate performance, and in the best-case scenario aim to cover the whole of their energy consumption through clean energy self-generation or to offset their energy consumption through clean energy investments elsewhere. The understanding is still to kick in that public services can, and will have to, become pillars of and leaders in the energy transition, if states around the world are to overhaul the global economic and energy system in line with the climate imperatives for 2050. By means of setting examples, diffusing best practices, showcasing the necessity and superiority of clean energy solutions across the environmental–economic–social nexus, and producing surplus energy quantities to accelerate the energy transition, public services can go a long way to take a pioneering role in the climate battlefield. What is at stake, ultimately, is that public services not only become carbon-neutral but also generate clean energy surpluses and make up carbon space for other actors and, very importantly, future generations.

Summary

Taking climate change and public services' endeavour to adjust to the mounting need for a comprehensive energy transition to achieve increasingly bold climate goals as an example, this chapter examined public services as actors in a changing world. It singled out three main policy competences of public services actors, namely goal- and agenda-setting, and *policy formulation* and *implementation*. Subsequently, it showcased several policy initiatives different public services have undertaken, such as setting goals and action plans, *regulatory* provisions, strategic investments in infrastructure, and strategic public procurement.

On this basis, the chapter has assessed the extent to which public services have successfully adjusted to the new disruptive reality and the needs of a changing economic landscape and showed that, on the one hand, several initiatives are in the right direction. On the other hand, nevertheless, the lack of a sense of urgency, of innovative solutions at scale and of a more comprehensive effort to upscale climate performance, have inevitably led to a sizeable gap between the needs of an economy under energy transition and public services actors' energy and climate performance. The challenge ahead for public services actors is to explore synergies across the social–economic–environmental nexus and examine potentials for collaboration. Ultimately, public services cannot afford simply to adapt; they need to become an enabler and accelerator of mitigation, of change and innovation.

Lastly, several factors render an increasing role for public services in the energy transition both more feasible and more pressing. From developments at the global climate governance level since the 2015 Paris Agreement, changing market fundamentals and the collapse of clean energy costs, to mounting civil society pressure and more scientific clarity and urgency, there is a clear trend towards and demand for more solidly embedding energy transition goals into the public services policy design and *policy implementation*.

Key points

- Environmental considerations are no longer second to social and economic parameters.
- Public services can influence the energy transition through their agenda- and goal-setting, *policy formulation* and *policy implementation* competences.
- Public services have taken up measures to improve their climate performance.
- A comprehensive understanding of the urgency of the climate challenge and of the scale of the energy transition needed remains lacking.
- Climate imperatives, civil society pressure, and changing political and market fundamentals create pressure and conducive ground for public services to take up a comprehensive energy transition agenda.
- Public services need to free carbon space for less privileged groups and future generations.

Questions

- How do environmental, social and economic factors interact in decision making?
- What are the main competences of public services through which they can contribute to the energy transition?
- What are the main activities public services have embarked upon to improve their climate performance? Do you consider them adequate/successful?
- What further actions can public services take to improve their climate performance and contribute to the energy transition?

> • Which factors render it easier/more important for public services actors to take environmental aspects more seriously in their decision-making processes?

Further reading

Denis, G. and Parker, P. (2009) 'Community energy planning in Canada: The role of renewable energy', *Renewable and Sustainable Energy Reviews,* 13(8): 2088–2095. *This article examines how energy communities in Canada drive the energy transition in distinct ways.*

Geels, F., Sovacool, B., Schwanen, T. and Sorrell, S. (2017) 'Sociotechnical transitions for deep decarbonization', *Science,* 357(6357): 1242–1244. *This article unpacks the multiple dimensions of decarbonization and shows how system approaches can contribute to the energy transition.*

Hoppe, T., van der Vegt, A. and Stegmaier, P. (2016) 'Presenting a framework to analyze local climate policy and action in small and medium-sized cities', *Sustainability,* 8(847). *This article examines the drivers for climate action in small and medium-sized cities.*

Strachan, P., Cowell, R., Ellis, G., Sherry-Brennan, F. and Toke, D. (2015) 'Promoting community renewable energy in a corporate energy world', *Sustainable Development,* 23(2): 96–109. *This article examines and accounts for the slow pace of renewables uptake at a community level in the UK.*

References

Daly, H. (1996) *Beyond growth: The economics of sustainable development,* Boston: Beacon Press.

Falkner, R. (2016) 'The Paris Agreement and the new logic of international climate politics', *International Affairs,* 92(5): 1107–1125.

IPCC (2019) *Special report: Global warming of 1.5 °C. Glossary,* available at: https://www.ipcc.ch/sr15/chapter/glossary/ [Accessed 25 January 2022].

Jackson, T. (1996) *Material concerns: Pollution, profit, and quality of life,* London: Routledge.

Mocatta, G. and White, R. (2020) 'This is how universities can lead climate action', *The Conversation,* 19 October, available at: https://theconversation.com/this-is-how-universities-can-lead-climate-action-147191 [Accessed 25 January 2022].

Ostrom, E. (2009) 'A polycentric approach for coping with climate change', *World Bank Policy Research Working Paper,* 5095.

Stern, N. (2006) *The economics of climate change: The Stern review,* Cambridge: Cambridge University Press.

Van de Graaf, T. and Sovacool, B. (2020) *Global Energy Politics,* Cambridge: Polity Press.

Wagner, O., Berlo, K., Herr, C. and Companie, M. (2021) 'Success factors for the foundation of municipal utilities in Germany', *Energies,* 14(4): 981.

Conclusion: Current developments and the future of public services

Elizabeth Cookingham Bailey, E.K. Sarter, Wendy Booth, Vida Greaux, Stuart Jones, Jennifer Law, David Phillips, Filippos Proedrou and Simon Read

Public services encompass a broad range of services, which are provided by or on behalf of the state to address vital needs and safeguard rights. They are embedded in a specific context and shaped by their sociopolitical and cultural surroundings, historical legacies, legal frameworks, technological changes, and ongoing and emerging developments. Before exploring the challenges that the continuously changing environment presents for public services, it seems vital to briefly recapitulate the main developments and trends which have been identified across the chapters of this book. Some core streams of developments can be distinguished.

First, the past few decades and years have seen important structural changes. The past decades have seen changes in the delegation of power to different levels of government, namely on the one hand a trend towards increasing supranational regulation and integration, and the empowerment of lower levels of government in several countries on the other. In terms of policy content, a second important change was the growing importance of environmental concerns and sustainability and an increasing awareness of the importance of equality and public services' equality impact. Further important changes include public administration reforms, which went along with the notion of the small state, increased constraints for public spending and an increasing marketisation of public services. This has been coupled with the increased usage of technology to deliver public services in the form of e-governance. In this context, public services delivery has increasingly been provided by a mix of different sectors.

To provide services that can adapt and respond to these developments, public services need to revisit their ways of working. The response to these changes needs to be guided by strong, forward-looking leadership and management. This requires leaders who engage in long-term planning within their organisations and anticipate the unexpected. Strategic leaders and managers need to develop strong situational awareness around the issues impacting their communities and the world. To do this, leaders must ensure they have strong communication skills and engage in reflective practices to improve their service delivery. This will be essential for work within and outside of the organisation. Inside the organisation the use of design thinking and compassionate leadership means that leaders engage and empower staff to develop innovative changes. Alongside this, managers encourage greater collaboration across services and sectors, allowing more flexibility in engagement with service users. The combination of the ability to collaborate and move between sectors requires public service organisations that are more fluid and public servants who are flexible, adaptable and compassionate. This allows public services to be ready for the 21st century. In the following the trends and developments will be examined further before exploring the implications for public services in more detail.

Recent, current and future challenges and changes

Changing balance of power among different political levels

Since the beginning of the 20th century, the world has changed significantly. Struggles for sovereignty have seen nations, particularly in the Global South, successfully gaining independence. From the founding of the United Nations (UN) to European integration, international and regional cooperation has increased significantly. International law impacts the national and subnational level (see Chapter 3), and regional integration exerts an impact on policymaking at national and subnational level – particularly but not exclusively in the European Union (EU).

The past few decades have seen two major developments relating to the balance of power. On the one hand, supranational coordination has become an increasingly important feature. Since the beginning of the 20th century, a range of supranational institutions and organisations, from the UN and its agencies to the Organisation for Economic Co-operation and Development (OECD) and the EU, were founded to promote supranational coordination, cooperation and regulation. A supranational legal framework has been established that interacts with and increasingly influences national and subnational laws and policies (see Chapter 3). Consequently, supranational cooperation and integration have gained growing importance, especially for the member states of the EU. This means that international law and policy play an important role in establishing the boundaries of public service action. Further supranational involvement, for instance in the form of supranational regulations on public procurement (which also apply to the purchase of services by public authorities, see Chapter 7) or climate change (see Chapter 10), has gained considerable importance for public services.

On the other hand, different countries have moved towards rebalancing the relationship between supranational and domestic decision making in favour of the latter. Internal political debates in some nation states have increasingly questioned an international or regional collectivist approach to decision making and advocated a focus on sovereignty and national decision making. In some cases, this has led to a shift towards less supranational integration. The most prominent example of this development was the British exit from the EU (Brexit), which has resulted in a shift towards more domestic and less supranational policymaking (see Chapters 1 and 3).

In addition to contrasting developments relating to supranational cooperation, coordination and regulation, the past decades have also seen debates on the distribution of power and the relationship between the national and subnational levels. In this context, different countries, such as the UK or France, have seen a shifting balance of power between the national and subnational level. Countries (particularly those that previously were heavily centralised) saw an increasing involvement and importance of subnational levels with a devolution of power, administration and control to local or regional governments, described as decentralisation (France) or devolution (UK) (see Chapters 1 and 3). While these developments delegate more power to subnational levels, they do not put into question the integrity of the respective nation states. Yet over the past decades in different countries, movements emerged, or grew stronger, that advocate for the creation of independent states, leading in some cases (for instance in Scotland or the French Territoire d'outre mer of Kanaky/Nouvelle Calédonie) to referenda being called on this issue (see Chapter 1).

These changes are brought into sharp focus with global issues. Climate change is one issue which has global impacts and requires global cooperation and solutions. Likewise, the COVID-19 pandemic has highlighted the importance of supranational cooperation and solidarity, in this specific case as one important strategy to face the challenges posed to healthcare systems. In the EU, solidarity among member states has been one feature of a coordinated response. In different instances, individual member states' requests for help led to medical staff from another member state coming to support their colleagues at different stages of the pandemic. Patients from countries and regions that were at the time particularly hard hit were treated in other countries to relieve the pressure on healthcare systems in their country of residence. These and other global issues have highlighted the important role of supranational cooperation and supranational organisations in setting benchmarks and coordinating best practice for public services to develop strategies while also greatly relying on localism to adapt responses to local circumstances and coordinate public service responses on the ground. The need for (and in some parts political will to further) supranational cooperation must thereby be reconciled with calls for more regional autonomy and, in some countries, movements that aim for independence.

Domestically, several countries have seen a change in the role of the state and the mode of governance. Of particular importance for Europe was the rise of the regulatory state, which uses rulemaking as a key mode of governance (see Chapter 1), as well as a turn towards ideas of a *small state*. This went along with increasing concerns about public budgets and increasing pressures to restrict public spending and borrowing, labelled as austerity (see Chapters 4 and 7). Within nation states, ideological and economic factors have driven a repositioning of the role of the public sector, with important consequences for public services, which, by definition, rely on public funding. This is driving changing ideas around how public services are led and managed which impact on the internal organisational culture. Several countries are, therefore, moving towards a smaller state approach with limitations on the size of the public sector and changes in how public services operate.

In addition to these structural changes, the content of policies, which set aims and goals for public services (see Chapter 1), has changed as new issues emerged, and other issues have become increasingly important for public services (though not exclusively). Equality is increasingly important; this also means considering the impact of public services on the wide range of users and seeking to account for their different needs (see Chapter 8). Environmental concerns, and climate change most prominently, have become more and more important topics on the political agenda and in public policies. Consequently, public services are increasingly called upon to assess their environmental impact and re-envision their practices (see Chapters 9 and 10). Alongside environmental considerations, sustainability, a multidimensional concept that integrates economic, environmental and social aspects, has become an increasingly important idea. The drive to more sustainable practices, which has been promoted at different levels, also relates to public service practices (see Chapter 7).

Overall, public services are operating in a changing environment, which has seen the emergence of new actors and institutions, a growth of supranational cooperation and regulation, and shifts in the balance of power between different levels. This has led to the expansion of regulation, policies and initiatives, and standards set by a variety of actors on different levels. This ever more complex web of regulations is thereby coupled with growing expectations to contribute to broader approaches and aims like taking on an active role in mitigating environmental challenges, fostering equality and developing more sustainable practices.

Changes in public service management in response to political change

The past decades have furthermore been characterised by public administration reforms in many countries. One of the main approaches is New Public Management (NPM). NPM is best understood as the integration of private sector management techniques into a public sector context and has important implications for public services. In their quest for efficiency and following the idea that the introduction of business techniques and competition would lead to increased efficiency and reduced spending, many states withdrew, at least partially, from the direct provision of services. Among Western welfare states, increased marketisation of services was a 'common reform strategy' (Veggeland, 2008: 280).

One of the main forms of *marketisation* comes in the form of contracting out of services, which were formerly provided by the public sector services, to voluntary and private providers (see Chapters 2 and 4). Marketisation has significantly increased public contracting of services, whereby a public authority buys a specific service from an external provider who subsequently delivers the service in exchange for public money (see Chapter 7). The impact of the underlying ideas of NPM has exerted an important influence beyond the reach of those countries who, like the UK, follow this approach. While contracting out, for instance, was 'a main dish on the NPM menu' (Pollitt and Bouckaert,

2011: 24), it was also 'used as a side dish' (Pollitt and Bouckaert, 2011: 24) in countries that followed other reform strategies. The increasing contracting out of services also means that public services are increasingly provided by a range of different sector organisations, which challenges the idea that a specific *public sector ethos* dominates the way frontline workers in public services approach the services. This is driving the creation of a separate *public service ethos* that would transcend the culture of any one sector that dominates different providers' approaches to the delivery of public services (Chapter 4). In the UK, this has led the Public Administration Select Committee to recommend the creation of a specific public service code in their seventh report (2002), much like the existing principles of public life introduced for the public sector by the Committee on Standards in Public Life (1995).

The provision of public services by non-public providers, who deliver these services on behalf of the state, is not a new phenomenon (see Introduction and Chapter 2). However, non-public providers are increasingly involved in the delivery of public services because of public administration reforms and the aligned marketisation of services. With an increased importance of contracting out of services, public procurement (defined as the purchase of goods, works and services by public bodies) has gained importance not only for safeguarding the availability of public services but also as a tool for regulating working conditions and standards (Chapter 7).

The usage of alternative non-state providers also presents new challenges. Partnerships allow for new expertise and increase economies of scale, but challenge more bureaucratic systems based on hierarchy and control. This requires considerations of principal-agent theory (see Chapter 7) and different power dynamics within partnerships. It furthermore challenges public service leaders and managers, who will need to work outside of previously set structures. Project-based approaches that draw across teams in organisations and across different public services are needed to tackle the extent of new risks and wicked issues (see Chapter 1), which requires a clear understanding of the strengths of each organisation drawing on a *resource-based approach* (see Chapter 5). Having this understanding allows for strategic positioning to compete for or share resources among the range of new providers. Managers must develop a strong situational awareness (see Chapter 6) which integrates understanding of both external and internal forces that impact organisations (see Chapters 4 and 5).

This is coupled with the usage of techniques within public services that draw on private sector techniques and ideas of transactional leadership, which is driven by a *carrot and stick* approach (see Chapter 6). It involves monitoring of external relationships with partners delivering services and internally with frontline staff (see Chapter 7) and fits in with core ideas around accountability and holding partners and frontline service workers to account for actions (see Chapter 4). At the same time, the public sector is taking a more regulatory function by checking on compliance with contracts, which can also involve tracking results and providing the opportunity for sharing learning between providers (see

Chapter 4). As new issues, such as environmental concerns or the drive to increase sustainability (see Chapters 7 and 9), gain importance for public policies and initiatives, they also become essential considerations of public sector organisations in the development or improvement of existing programmes, services, buildings and essential resources. Providers can show achievement against targets in relation to sustainability and shared learning around addressing environmental issues.

Alongside movements to increase accountability through targets, efforts have also been introduced to increase service user choice and involvement in the direction of public services. This again draws on techniques utilised by the private sector. It also brings an increasing need for new communication techniques to facilitate that engagement. Public services have been encouraged to work with local communities to identify local and community needs and gaps in services, and to account for different needs (see Chapter 8). Voluntary sector providers are an important partner as they frequently have access to communities that may be missed by or hard to access for the public sector (see Chapter 2). Sharing of expertise is an asset to the development of public services, but also requires shifting existing policy, strategy and decision-making processes (see Chapters 1 and 5). The integration of a wider variety of views in decision making is also dependent on the timeframe available, as not all public service changes may have the adequate time allotted.

Technological change: challenges and opportunities

Over the past few decades, more widespread access to and an increasing use of digital technologies, and the internet more specifically, has been a common development, which opens new ways for thinking about and delivering public services, particularly under the conditions of increasing collaboration. These new digital technologies open the opportunity for e-governance (see Chapter 4) and serve dual functions of increasing distribution of information, encouraging engagement and providing online alternatives to traditional physical in-person options.

Technological changes have also partially taken place to address the increased need for accountability and transparency in public services. Regular data reporting against targets and in terms of achievement of milestones in long-term strategies has increased (see Chapters 4 and 5). The transparency produced by this data allows more scrutiny of public service organisations and can also be used to shape funding opportunities. Increased need for data has also encouraged public service organisations to include more first-hand experiences of service users as part of that reporting, which can improve the equality impact (see Chapter 8).

With internet access and use more and more widespread, public services are increasingly shifting to virtual services or complementing their in-person provision with digital services. The growing importance of digital technologies in general and the digital provision of services more specifically has also been driven by a wider range of sectors involved in service delivery (see Chapter 2). This could include the option of paying for services through online portals rather than going to physical locations or the usage of telehealth or e-health. The use of digital technologies and e-governance can be seen to overlay against all of Arnstein's (1969) levels and can be a core tool to increase service user engagement in public services. At the most basic level, it opens a space for therapy for service users to express dissatisfaction with services. It also provides users with information and some tokenistic consultation on selected issues. Most importantly, e-governance also provides the means of facilitating a high level of citizen engagement where citizens are given more control over services as they can be discussed and designed in collaboration easily and effectively. Working digitally can be a way of increasing transparency and running services in a cost-effective way. During the COVID-19 pandemic, when many countries experienced lockdowns, digital delivery of services also opened opportunities to comply with social distancing and lockdown requirements and added public health considerations to the benefits of digital opportunities. It has also accelerated the digital provision of services.

While e-governance can support co-production of services through virtual platforms and consultations and bring in service users with first-hand experiences to shape the direction of programmes in public service organisations and improve equality (see Chapters 4 and 8), it does not come without challenges. First, the initial creation of e-governance infrastructure can be quite costly to establish, but once integrated, provides an opportunity to streamline the efficiency in labour and finances of public services (see Chapter 4). In addition, the pandemic has also highlighted the differing impacts that a digital provision of services can generate. Digital provision relies on service users having secure internet connections, compatible devices frequently with functioning cameras and microphones, and private spaces in which to work. Not all households have access to multiple devices, which may require balancing access to services, such as health or education, against the needs of other household members to work remotely (see Chapter 4). At the same time, digital provision may raise further issues for certain users due to their specific situation.

Considering solutions

Public services are facing challenges from structural changes relating to the influence of different political levels, changing ideological views about how services should be delivered and managed, and changing technologies. Adding to these are the challenges created by the emergence of new considerations such as sustainability or the mitigation of environmental developments and climate change (see Chapters 7, 9 and 10). The urgency of the environmental crisis and the many complex elements are one pull on public service resources. To tackle the variety of challenges presented by the environmental crisis public services need to be prepared to respond to urgent crises. They also need to engage in a broader strategy which is likely to be set at a national or supranational level. However, public service actors are a key element in this discussion because of the impact the services themselves have on the environment and climate change more specifically. Public services can contribute by modelling action, by increasing knowledge on how to tackle issues (see Chapter 9) and by taking part in the larger energy transition (see Chapter 10). Alongside this, public services need to adjust for changing demographics which impact on the number of people contributing to the work-based economy, leading to consequent changes in funding. They must also understand the resulting different demands on public services across the life course, which change based on issues like migration and ageing societies (see Chapter 4). This highlights the continual challenge of public services providing services that promote equality and diversity. The services must recognise the different and competing needs of populations that may fluctuate over time by engaging in service delivery innovation. Like tackling climate change, this requires a long-term perspective.

All of this creates new challenges as these additional considerations for and demands on public services require staff knowledge about long-term planning that balances competing factors when not trained in these areas, which is another aspect that might be particularly challenging for managers and leaders who may have come up in the organisation with the core frontline skills, but without awareness of larger contextual factors. Second, it requires additional work to ensure existing and new public service elements comply with sustainability measures set out by governments, which means that additional resources are required. This further contributes to competing economic, political and social forces shaping public services (see Chapters 4, 5 and 7).

To deal with these changes and address current and future demands, strategic planning is vital. Increasing evidence suggests that it leads to improved performance for public service organisations (see Chapter 5). Strategic planning depends on identifying and assessing issues and trends and their implications, and provides a mechanism for managers to look at the context to explore both strong and weak signals from both the internal and the external environment. Without this, there is a danger that inappropriate strategies will be developed that have not considered the situation fully. Big data and forecasting can be essential tools to evaluate trends and assess their impacts. Some organisations are also using scenario planning to explore what the long-term future might look like and thereby engaging in conceptual innovation (Windrum, 2008). Public service leaders also need to embrace ideas of design thinking (see Chapter 6) in the way they address issues using innovative and iterative processes. This type of approach encourages a focus on the user experience (through qualitative and quantitative methods) and on innovating through developing and testing prototypes. This can also be supported by the ideas of compassionate leadership, which relies on leaders engaging in discussion and gaining insights from their team to build shared responsibility and vision. The combination of strategic planning, compassionate leadership and design thinking allows public services to adapt and engage in administrative innovation (Windrum, 2008) to tackle new and continuing challenges related to sustainability, equality and climate change.

Public services are also required to adopt new ways of working and engage in collaboration, partnership working and co-production. Public services have often relied on the bottom rung of Arnstein's (1969) ladder of participation, engaging in more manipulation and therapy in how they engage with users. While including citizens and users is not a new idea, previous practices and trends were more geared towards tokenistic one-way flows of communication, which evolved into two-way consultation with the public that still held an emphasis on placation. As noted earlier, technological change has the capacity to help ensure valuable high-level engagement, but it is more the nature of the issues on which public services are asking for input that can encourage true co-production. New challenges, such as climate change or the increasing attention given to the equality impact of public services, are demanding greater citizen power in decision making on public services, more partnership working, delegated power and control. Calls for a stronger inclusion of citizens, communities and service users are also driven by awareness of democratic deficit, the rise of evidence-based policy, greater transparency, and expectations about services by the public (Jones and Gammel, 2009). This growing need for and push towards collaboration, partnership working and co-production also means that the way public services work and engage with other organisations changes, requiring effective and successful management of change and challenges for leadership to effectively bring about systematic innovation.

One of the key challenges of both leadership and management in public services is the increasing need to collaborate between and across organisations and sectors. The principle of *interoperability*, the exchange and sharing of information, has become more commonplace in public service organisations. For example, in the UK, the emergency services have been exploring ways to lead more effective collaborations between the services. In 2013, a review was conducted of common failures impacting on interoperability, which included inadequate training, ineffective communication, lack of review systems, a lack of leadership and an embedded culture of blame (Pollock, 2013). This led to the adoption of a national strategy for all levels of command in emergency services that ensured lessons learned from incidents were identified and used to drive change. This forms part of the Joint Emergency Services Interoperability Principles utilised by public service leaders.

The future of public services and the 21st-century civil servant

Public services navigate an increasingly complex set of regulations, aims and expectations while at the same time facing stringent demands for efficiency, budgetary constraints and a quest to achieve more with less. This also means that techniques used across sectors draw on a variety of different providers to deliver services. Public servants are expected to engage in new ways of working and transcend old boundaries; they need to be flexible to take on new challenges, from taking an active role in promoting equality to being a part of attempts to mitigate the environmental crisis. To better understand (and be a part of) the communities in which they operate, public services are expected to engage in partnership working, incorporate users' perspectives, and engage with citizens, residents and communities in a co-productive way.

These changes and expectations raise demands for public services as organisations and redefine what it means to be a public servant regardless of sector. This has led to investigations of what it means to be a *21st century public servant* (Needham and Mangan, 2014). If public services are to take on new challenges, they must understand what the new expectations mean for public services and how they can best be addressed. This in turn raises demands for knowledge, innovation and, ultimately, in the implementation, the management of change. More collaboration and partnership working means that those engaged in these collaborations and partnerships need to have the knowledge, skills and capacity to work across sectors and move between sectors bridging the more commercial ideas of NPM and the older public-mindedness of classic welfare eras.

Overall, public servants will need to undertake a range of different roles and activities; they will effectively engage with citizens and possess soft skills, including but not limited to communication and caring skills. To master this challenging environment, reflective practice of public servants, public service workers, leaders and organisations themselves is crucial, and constant learning from others is essential. In this context, leadership has an important role to play; it needs to be collaborative and distributed rather than 'heroic' (Needham and Mangan, 2014: 6). Public service organisations need to provide effective support; they will need to be fluid and supportive, with organisational culture as one focal point of attention (Needham and Mangan, 2014).

Public services, and those who work in them, need to be adaptable, forward thinking, and attentive to both the local and the global communities of which they are a part. It is only by embracing a willingness to change, learn, collaborate and innovate that public services can meet the variety of challenges they now face, and those yet to come.

References

Arnstein, S. (1969) 'The ladder of citizen participation', *Journal of American Institute of Partners*, 35(4): 216–224.

Committee on Standards in Public Life (1995) *The seven principles of public life*, London: HMSO.

Jones, R. and Gammel, E. (2009) *The art of consultation: Public dialogues in a noisy world*, London: Biteback Publishing.

Needham, C. and Mangan, C. (2014) *The twentieth century public servant*, Birmingham: University of Birmingham.

Pollitt, C. and Bouckaert, G. (2011) *Public management reform: A comparative analysis – new public management, governance and the neo-Weberian state*, Oxford: Oxford University Press.

Pollock, K. (2013) *Review of persistent lessons identified relating to interoperability from emergencies and major incidents since 1986*, Emergency Planning College Occasional Paper New Series Number 6 2013.

Public Administration Select Committee (2002) *Select Committee on public administration seventh report*, London: HMSO.

Veggeland, N. (2008) 'Path dependence and public sector innovation in regulatory regimes', *Scandinavian Political Studies*, 31(3): 268–290.

Windrum, P. (2008) 'Innovation and entrepreneurship in public services', in Windrum, P. and Koch, P. (eds) *Innovation in public sector services: Entrepreneurship, creativity and management*, Cheltenham: Edward Elgar, pp 3–20.

Index

References to figures appear in *italic* type;
those in **bold** type refer to tables.